LUKE KELLY

A Memoir

Des Geraghty

A NOTE ON THE AUTHOR

Des Geraghty is a Dubliner from Cornmarket in the Liberties. He comes from a family which is steeped in the history, folklore and tradition of the city and has a special interest in traditional music and song. As a musician himself, he was a participant in the revival of interest in folk music in the '50s and '60s, as were Luke Kelly and his fellow-Dubliners. He is a well known trade unionist who has represented workers in most major industrial sectors in Ireland, and is currently a Democratic Left Member of the European Parliament, representing Dublin.

Basement Press
DUBLIN

DEDICATION

For my parents, Lily and Tom, who did so much to nurture in their sons a love of music and our own traditions; and my daughters, Maeve, Nóra and Eva, who carry on these traditions.

L28,052/782.0092

First published in Ireland in 1994 by
Basement Press
4 Upper Mount Street
Dublin 2

A catalogue record for this title is available from the British Library
ISBN 1 855940 906

Cover Design: Syd Bluett
Cover Photograph: Richard Dann
Origination: Verbatim Typesetting and Design
Printing: The Guernsey Press Co. Ltd.

CONTENTS

TRIBUTES TO LUKE KELLY

When Luke was singing a very good song, you could feel the hair rise on the back of your neck.

Peggy Seeger

I was amazed by the power and commitment of Luke's performance and by how emotionally involved he was with his material...He was a hero who became a friend and I still mourn him.

Christy Moore

Luke stood out as being passionate in his singing...he put soul into it.

Mary Coughlan

He was a hard chaw with a heart of gold and the soul of an angel.

Barney McKenna

He stood head and shoulders above the others...he gave a voice to the unemployed; he gave a voice to the worker; a voice to the person on the streets of Dublin.

Frank Harte

He had a quality impossible to define and certainly impossible to learn.

Phil Coulter

You couldn't help but respect Luke for his tremendous integrity and the way he stuck to his convictions throughout his life. As a singer, he was the best bar none.

Ronnie Drew

FOREWORD

There were no pictures of Luke Kelly on the walls of Laurence O'Toole's School. That privilege was preserved for the exceptions that reached some academic landmark – a degree, perhaps, or the calling to the priesthood. Yet Luke was a mould-breaker infinitely more out of the ordinary. Like many of his class he took the emigrant boat which was supposed to be a one-way journey to anonymity. If you did return it was in silence and without fanfare.

But Luke Kelly returned a hero, genuinely acclaimed and revered by the people of the North Wall. The home-coming party began in rooms above an off-licence in Whitworth Row – a street that nestled below the railway line that traversed Seville Place on its way north. The door and windows of the house were thrown open and the ensuing sing-song was at once private and public. Scores of youngsters and adults sat on the road late into the night, joining in choruses when they knew them, observing traditional Celtic order for the singer (one voice only) which invariably was the man himself. When bewildered newcomers or happy late-night stumblers enquired as to the origins of the impromptu street festival, they were met with a collective cry: 'Luke's home!'

It lasted a week. On successive nights, Sheriff Street's pubs played host: Bertie Donnelly's (by the corner of Guild Street), The Ball Alley that straddled Emerald Street, Noctor's that faced Clickey Murphy's lane and Doyle's Railway Bar that hung around Oriel Street. Each location was baptised with a round for the adults and a grush [a scatter of money] for the kids, a custom normally reserved for weddings. Well, it was a kind of

1

marriage, a re-bonding; in truth it was more a reclaiming. The prodigal son had returned to be adopted and exalted by his clan of origin.

It was strange, this chasm between community respect and official indifference. But then Luke Kelly was a socialist and there were no official socialist heroes in the Ireland of the 1950s and 1960s. Official Ireland had bought the red scare, hook, line and sinker. There is no more powerful controlling mechanism than fear, and the ruling classes perfected a diet of fear that was administered in every classroom in the land. The basic ingredients consisted of the communist threat from Russia (there were prayers for its conversion), mandatory corporal punishment (ordained by God, who punished for eternity), and the fear of socialism which sought to destroy God (the same one who loved us by beating us). We digested it well. As a result, we managed to preserve ourselves from the evils of James Joyce, Brendan Behan, Edna O'Brien, the *Kama Sutra*, the *Decameron*, Federico Fellini, John McGahern, J P Donleavy, Sean O'Casey and other heathen influences.

But they couldn't stop Luke singing. And no voice better railed against injustice, inhumanity and degradation. Forget the words – it was the passion. When Luke sang you stood shoulder to shoulder with your mates in the picket line, or you felt the inexpressible grief of unrequited love (as Paddy Kavanagh did in 'Raglan Road') or your perception of the disabled changed forever. Never again would simplicity be scorned. When Luke sang you felt ennobled. It was uplifting, a purifying moment. Through the grief in his voice, the pain, the love, he lifted experience out of the mundane and gave it nobility. It felt good to be working class. Better than that, it felt important. Better still, it could be expressed. The struggle was no longer suppressed. Through the medium of Luke we grasped that rare thing, unflinching solidarity, the thing that makes us invincible. His voice still rings in our ears. You can hear it perfectly; it is the clarion call of our rightful inheritance that can never be silenced.

Jim and Peter Sheridan, Spring 1994

PREFACE

I was greatly honoured when, in January 1993, Luke Kelly's brother, Jimmy, asked me to say a few words at Luke's grave. It was part of the commemoration that Jimmy organises each year. But I was also shocked to realise that already Luke was nine years dead and that in 1994 it would be a decade since he left us.

Writing those few words brought a flood of memories of Luke, going back to such places as O'Donoghue's pub, the Gate, The Grafton, the Embankment and Liberty Hall. More than that, it reminded me of that amazing era when song, music, the arts and the impetus for social change seemed to come together for a whole generation.

Jimmy and I were both involved in a workers' cultural organisation called *Scéim na gCeárdchumann* and we have remained good friends since. Like Luke, Jimmy is a remarkable ballad singer with a distinctive style and very strong delivery; he always evokes in me a memory of Luke.

Luke was Dublin's king when the young people of his city were beginning to release a pent-up energy and creativity which had been muted for a long time. He had a big voice, big enough to speak for all of us. He gave us, the Dubliners, pride in the sound of our own accent, in our own tradition; and a sense of joy, hope and determination about our future.

I believe that has been a lasting legacy through the troubled years since; and it seemed time that some attempt were made to salute his extraordinary contribution.

This book marks the tenth anniversary of Luke's tragically early death at the age of forty-three and I hope it goes some small way towards commemorating him.

5

ACKNOWLEDGMENTS

In putting this book together, I have drawn on my own recollections and those of so many others who knew Luke Kelly, who were moved and influenced by his work. It isn't possible to name them all, but I want to express my particular thanks first to Luke's family: his sisters, Bessie and Mona; his brothers, Paddy, Jimmy and John who shared rich memories of their childhood and teenage years in Sheriff Street and Whitehall; to Deirdre O'Connell; to Peggy Jordan and to Liam and Seamus Mulready; to Madeleine Seiler for talking to me about the years she and Luke shared; and to the members of The Dubliners, who spent much time recalling the early '60s in Dublin and London.

It has always been the hallmark of The Dubliners that no degree of success has in any way affected their warmth and openness, their ease with their home audience and their readiness for a chat or a session or both. I am especially grateful to John Sheahan for unstinting help and to Barney McKenna for his contribution, which came wrapped up in a couple of excellent sessions on his home ground of Howth; also to Ronnie Drew for his vivid recollections, recounted in his own inimitable style. I greatly appreciate Micheál Ó Caoimh's two extended taped interviews with Luke and his allowing us to use his ballad about Luke, and the help I received from the finest exponent of the Dublin street ballad, Frank Harte, who gave very generously of his own recollections and opinions, as well as making available a remarkable taped interview and session with Luke.

Everyone had their own stories to tell, but my special thanks are due to Phil Coulter, who went to great trouble in the middle of a busy schedule to talk to me at length about his personal and professional friendship with Luke; to Gerry Fleming, who has a total and lively recall of the way we were; to Declan Collinge for his poems; to Eamon Campbell, Eric Fleming, Bill Whelan, Ted McKenna, Seán Redmond, Máirín Johnston, Paddy Gillan, Barbara Kelly, Bruce Dunnett, Hayden Murphy, Dessie Carmichael, Martin Glennon, Peggy Seeger, Christy Moore, Mary Coughlan, Rosheen Callender and Janie Buchan, MEP for Glasgow, all of whom made their own special contribution; and especially to Mary Maher, who gave invaluable assistance in research and editing, as well as contributing her own vivid memories of the '60s in Dublin. Without her help, this book would not have been possible.

Thanks are also due to my own family, brothers and close relatives who remember Luke so well, and particularly my brother Sean who so often shared a pint with Luke in London and took many photographs of times they spent together.

As well as many newspaper cuttings, other sources of valuable information were *The Dubliners' Scrapbook* by Mary Hardy (London: Wise Publications, 1978); *Journeyman* by Ewan MacColl (London: Sidgwick and Jackson, 1990); and *Bringing it All Back Home* by Nuala O'Connor (London: BBC Books, 1991).

For What Died the Sons of Róisín

Luke Kelly

For what died the sons of Róisín, was it fame?
For what died the sons of Róisín, was it fame?
For what flowed Ireland's blood in rivers
That began when Brian chased the Dane,
And did not cease, nor has not ceased
With the brave sons of '16
For what died the sons of Róisín, was it fame?

For what died the sons of Róisín, was it greed?
For what died the sons of Róisín, was it greed?
Was it greed that drove Wolfe Tone to a pauper's
   death
In a cell of cold wet stone,
Will German or French or Dutch
Inscribe the epitaph of Emmet
When we have sold enough of Ireland
To be but strangers in it?
For what died the sons of Róisín, was it greed?

To whom do we owe our allegiance today?
To whom do we owe our allegiance today?
To those brave men who fought and died
That Róisín live again with pride,
Her sons at home to work and sing
Her youth to dance and make her valleys ring,
Or the faceless men who for mark and dollar
Betray her to the highest bidder.
To whom do we owe our allegiance today?

For what suffer our patriots today?
For what suffer our patriots today?

9

They have a language problem – so they say –
How to trespass must grieve their heart full sore.
We got rid of one strange language
Now we are faced with many more
For what suffer our patriots today?

From *Arena* Broadsheet Five,
produced by Hayden Murphy

CHAPTER ONE

A new poetry is slowly breathing its way to life.
Suffering is opening the poet's eyes even though
tradition ties his tongue. We must patiently await
the utterance.

Leslie Daiken, introduction to
Goodbye Twilight, 1936

Luke Kelly and I were both born about one mile from
O'Connell Street, on opposite sides of the Liffey, and the
Dublin we grew up in during the 1940s and 1950s was a
greyer and drearier place than anyone who has known it
only since that far-off time might believe. Luke described
it simply and succinctly many years later, in 1967, at the
height of his early success with The Dubliners, when he
said in an interview: 'There's a new spirit among young
people, a political and social awareness that I think is
directly related to the ballads...the movement has had a
definite liberalising effect. I grew up in a dead city; I
don't think it's dead now. I think things are going to
happen in Ireland again...'

At that time the fantastic success of what was known
to us as 'the ballad movement' was beginning to suffer
the negative effects of commercialisation, and Luke,
while not denying that some of the songs had become
devalued and removed from their original intent, argued
that the movement had had positive effects that hadn't
reached their full potential yet: 'The music has suffered,
but there have been compensations. It's a dialectical
question,' he said, in a typical Luke Kelly response.

That deadness he referred to of 'Dublin in the rare old
times' was partly, but not wholly, a product of our
common environment: poverty. Certainly as a child I

assumed everyone as poor. I don't think we knew anyone who had any money, except publicans and shopkeepers, and in retrospect I don't think they had an awful lot either. I've no doubt there was a wealthy merchant class in Dublin in those days but its members had long since headed for the greener pastures of the well-to-do suburbs. They had deserted the inner city and left its magnificent Georgian houses, ranging proudly along Mountjoy Square, Gardiner Street, Henrietta Street, to degenerate into rundown tenements for the lower orders.

The only differentiation you could make was between degrees of poverty. In Cornmarket in the Liberties we were considered lucky because we had the distinction of having a locked hall door, whereas the other tenement house alongside us had an open hall door. Behind that gaping doorway were large numbers of people, the old and frail, the young, whole families crammed into small rooms, who had to put up with the single tap in the yard and open toilets that very often were stinking and unusable.

Luke knew the same scenes. In 1967 he also gave a long interview to the *Irish Socialist* and his reply to the sweeping question: 'What is your ambition for your native city, and for Ireland?' speaks volumes. He said: 'I want to see its best qualities preserved, that is, its historically and aesthetically valuable parts. I would like to see the obverse of this in the abolition of every mouldy, seedy, and uninhabitable dwelling and to do this you have to give priority to the extirpation of private – and of capitalist necessity, vicious – landlordism.'

Luke was born on 17 November 1940 (his birth certificate says December 17, but his mother always maintained it was a month out, and the family agreed that she should know) in exactly that kind of uninhabitable dwelling: Lattimore Cottages on Sheriff Street, a form of 19th-century accommodation which in those days abounded in Dublin and isn't entirely gone yet: a

12

collection of eight or so single-storey buildings with two rooms, outside toilet and a single tap in the yard to be shared by all. Luke's mother, Julia Fleming, grew up in Lattimore Cottages. Her mother, who lived with the family until her death in 1953, was a MacDonald and the Kellys believe she came from Scottish stock, which may explain something of the affinity Luke always had for Scottish songs.

The Kellys moved in with Luke's grandmother when they married and the children were born in the cottage. In 1942, when the authorities finally got around to demolishing Lattimore Cottages, they became the first family to be housed in St Laurence O'Toole flats, where they lived on the Mayor Street side. Like so many thousands of Dublin families, their means were meagre and their prospects extremely limited, but that did not deter them from enjoying themselves and each other's company. The Kellys are a close and loyal tribe, and none of Luke's meteoric success in the '60s and '70s affected their relationships with one another.

Luke was himself always notably reticent about discussing his family, guarding his private life carefully during the years when his followers were avid for information about him. But they tell stories about him which are typical of his good nature and generosity – that the first paycheque he ever earned, for £25 in 1963, went to buy a pram for his sister Bessie's first child, Paula McCann; and that when in Dublin he frequently sang for the Legion of Mary in Regina Coeli Hall, where his sister Mona was a volunteer, arriving at 8 pm and giving them an hour-long concert before he tore off to appear on stage. In October 1970, Luke flew home for the day for Mona's wedding. Unfortunately, Richard Nixon was arriving in Ireland on the same day and the security delays at the airport meant that he missed the ceremony. He made it to the hotel, spent the afternoon with his family, and was back on a flight to London that night.

Luke regularly came out to his mother for Saturday or

Sunday dinner, drinking the dose of cabbage-water Dublin mothers of that generation set so much store by for health. There are funny stories, too, such as the time a taximan ferrying passengers away from a Dubliners' concert chanced to make a disparaging remark about 'That Luke Kelly one', and was promptly ordered to stop by the small woman next to him who turned out to be Luke's mother. Even today, Luke's brothers and sisters are close friends and time spent in their company usually consists of telling yarns and laughing.

Dublin never suffered from impoverishment of the spirit. Far from it. This had everything to do with the triumph of humanity, and, sad to say, owed nothing to any encouragement received from those institutions which were the other deadening influences on our lives. The three pillars of the Irish establishment – the Church, the State and the employers – were virtually unchallenged in their absolute authority, and enjoyed power which is, in retrospect, scarcely credible.

The conservative Catholic hierarchy had successfully resisted the 'insidious' threat to Catholic school teaching inherent in the concept of the welfare state, which might have the State doing for individuals what they should do for themselves. In practice, this meant the substitution of charitable works and clerical control of health, education and welfare for the proper system of universal entitlement which was rapidly becomming the norm in most of western Europe.

There was however a handful of courageous public figures, of whom Noel Browne is the prime example. The plan which he tried valiantly to put into effect during the 1940s for the poor women of Dublin and their babies was crushed beneath the crozier, denounced because it might have introduced the dangerous notion that the State had an obligation to look after its infant citizens. All this at a time when the Irish maternal and obstetric mortality rates were amongst the highest in the world, and where, as my mother recalled, a woman having a baby in the Coombe hospital could expect to sleep on the bare rubber mattress with a half-sheet of linen tucked on top of the blanket to look respectable for the Master doing his daily rounds. This was the kind of reality that underpinned the apparently absolute authority of the Church, and in my view gave rise to a dual morality, the publicly pious and privately rebellious nature of Irish Catholicism.

The State presided over persistently high levels of unemployment, emigration, poverty and poor housing conditions, while the leaders of the nation basked in the warmth of the Celtic twilight, which honoured, along with comely maidens, an insular and exclusive moral superiority and declared but remote national objectives of restoring the Irish language and reuniting the island of Ireland. For the majority of Dubliners, all this was quite unreal. Survival was the name of the game of life, and there was little room left for sanctimonious humbug. In any case, this brand of patriotism in no way inhibited the activities of the new Catholic business class whose position had been secured by the foundation of the State, and the property-owning class; both were busy marketing the comely maiden's honour to the highest bidder, selling any bit of the country they could lay their hands on. Was it any wonder that Luke Kelly would later compose the lines of *For what died the sons of Róisín?* with such power and venom:

'Will German, French or Dutch inscribe
The epitaph of Emmet?
When we have sold enough of Ireland
To be but strangers in it?'

The same sentiments were expressed vividly in another favourite of Luke's, Robert Burns's *Such a Parcel of Rogues in a Nation*:

'But we're bought and sold for English gold
Such a parcel of rogues in a nation...'

Identification with workers and the generally dispossessed was a constant characteristic of Luke's songs throughout his singing career, and it came from his own roots. The working-class communities of Dublin were small close-knit worlds, where people depended on each other because there was no one else to turn to. Luke's brother, Paddy, talking about the hardship that was the norm, recalled that the major Saturday morning chore in those years was getting the turf. Mrs Kelly's widowed mother had the voucher, and Paddy and Luke had the weekly task of setting off with a box-cart to collect a hundredweight of turf from the Ballybough depot. 'But there were always a few others, widows around us, who'd ask would we mind collecting for them as well. We'd be standing down there in the freezing cold shed sometimes for three hours, between one load getting delivered and then waiting for another. Then we'd start back again, and I will always remember staggering up Portland Row with a huge load of soaking wet turf on the cart between us.'

We even relied on our own local sources of information. News of distant parts, for instance, was generally imparted by a group known with affection as 'the lads at the corner'. The lads had travelled, seen some of the world. Some had worked abroad for a period, and on returning were enjoying restful days holding up the corners on the streets of Dublin. Quite a lot had returned from the ranks of the British army and had been serving all over the world. There was always a link between the Dublin working-class and the British army, as there was between people from around the port of Dublin and the merchant navy. That was a very strong tradition although it has become less and less significant in recent times.

When the lads came home again, they were very authoritative on the wars in the Far and Middle East, food and climate in foreign parts and a range of other subjects. Some were experts on football, the price of

Guinness, public affairs and political chicanery; they were our commentators on things of the day. If the circumstances were right and they had the price of a pint, they could occasionally burst into song, curse and swear with the best, tell yarns or fantasise about what James McKenna called in *The Scatterin'*, his powerful play about the 1950s, 'a happy land, far, far away'.

There seemed to be a nucleus of the lads that was perpetually unemployed, though quite a number might come and go, getting part-time work in Guinness's, the docks or in some of the local warehouses. The employers of Dublin we were most familiar with were those who took on casual labour. Dublin was never a manufacturing city, so most employment was in the services, or the transport and warehousing sector, in coal or cattle. Men depended on these, or on the Corporation, for a few hours' or a few days' work. The women got work in the small clothing factories that dotted the inner city or in the likes of Jacobs' biscuit factory.

However, given the lack of money, we did make our own fun. We had a great interest in, almost an obsession with, football. Soccer was the great game of the street. We all went to Christian Brothers' schools and played Gaelic and hurling. I think the youngsters of the city of Dublin were the avant garde, breaking the GAA ban on foreign games. We didn't make distinctions between Gaelic and foreign; those were the impositions of our betters, subtle categorisations that made no sense in a city without any sports facilities worth talking about.

Dealing with the gardai was much more relevant to us. I find it extraordinary now to remember how much time we spent running away from coppers (or bobbies, or rossers) who were constantly on the look-out to catch us playing street football. That was our early introduction to the majesty of the law, and what we encountered was a predominantly rural force that had no sympathy with the gurriers of Dublin. It was reasonable for us to believe, as we did, that street football was the only major

17

crime that concerned the gardai. They were very skilled at hunting down the criminals, enthusiastic in chasing, arresting and even charging kids whose mothers then had to find someone to mind the younger children and allow them to go down to court. We became equally skilled at evading the hunters, but learned to harbour a deep hostility to all manifestations of law and order.

Whatever else about the life, it did develop a great survival instinct among the young on the streets. I suppose it was that survival instinct that gave so many the grit to go on and make good lives even though poorly equipped in terms of education and material goods.

Luke Kelly senior had better material circumstances than many: he had a permanent job in Jacobs', where he was a member of the Amalgamated Transport and General Workers' Union. He worked there for more than forty-five years, from the time he was a boy, and met Luke's mother there. Luke's paternal grandfather was from Athlone – reputedly born next door to John McCormack – but came to Dublin and ended up on Marlborough Place. Luke's father grew up there, around the corner from my mother on Marlborough Street. He had an eventful enough young life, including the distinction of being the youngest victim of the Howth gun-running episode, after he was accidentally caught in a volley of shots from the King's Own Scottish Borderers on Bachelor's Walk. He survived to become one of Dublin's best young footballers, playing for Wasps and Jacobs, and had he been just a few inches taller, he would have had a professional career in the sport. He was also an extraordinary swimmer, something his children remember vividly. According to Luke's sister Bessie: 'If we were coming home from town and he took it into his head to go for a swim, nothing would do him but to dive into the Liffey.' He often swam from Butt Bridge past the shipping sheds, with Paddy carrying his clothes, or as far as the North Wall if he was in form.

One of the few anecdotes Luke told about his father concerned his swimming prowess. In an interview with Joe McAnthony, Luke talked of the terror he felt standing on the quayside watching him swim out of sight. He followed that up with a gleeful story about his father as a young man undertaking for a bet to swim across the Liffey with his hat on. He won the bet and was arrested for his trouble, the escapade resulting in the alarmist headline: 'Well-known footballer arrested for suicide attempt.'

By all the accounts of those who knew him, Luke Kelly senior was a gentle man – 'He wouldn't allow us to raise our voices at home', Bessie said – as well as an old-fashioned gentleman, 'a man who always tipped his hat to you,' according to Paddy's wife, Breda. He was also a strong family man, and Bessie said they were the only family in the flats who were taken to the seaside, to Portmarnock or Dollymount, on a daily basis during their father's annual summer leave. 'We went off every day, my mother with a big shopping bag with her loaves of bread and jam or beetroot and my father with a few sticks and the kettle, and everyone saying 'Oh, the Kellys are off again...' This compensated the children for the envy they felt at school when the rest of their classmates were queuing up with forms filled out for holidays at the Sunshine Homes, for which the Kellys, with a father in permanent employment, didn't qualify. L28.052/782.0092

Paddy and Luke did get a fortnight's holiday every year in Meath, by virtue of being members of O'Connell Boys Clubs. They were both ardent footballers. 'What you'd remember most about Luke was that he was football crazy,' Bessie said. 'He played football every weekend, and I have a clear memory of him coming home once and telling my father he'd played against a fellow named Johnny Giles who was definitely going to go places.' Luke remained a dedicated follower of soccer all his life, and Paddy tells a story related to an Ireland–England match which Ireland was winning with half a minute to go. 'In those days in Ireland we weren't a great footballing nation, so it was a great event,' he said. The fans had their white handkerchiefs out ready to wave when Tom Finney got the ball and buried it in the Irish net, leaving a hushed shock over Dalymount Park. Years later, who but Finney should be among those pressing forward to meet the famous Dubliners at a concert in Preston. Luke reported to his brother that when he met Tom Finney, he told him immediately 'I'll never forgive you, you bastard, for that day in Dalymount Park.'

But like the rest of us, Paddy and Luke had no difficulty switching from one nation's version of the game to another. Paddy played for Rathfarnham, cycling to the suburbs from Sheriff Street, and won a cap for Ireland in 1953. On Saturday afternoons he and Luke played GAA for O'Connell's, and on Sunday afternoon they played soccer. 'Luke was three years younger than I was but we played on the same team and he held his own,' Paddy said. 'He was always strong as a bull – though the da thought he was a bit too slow.' However, as Paddy said, 'He was a bit clever too.' Once in an inter-club tournament when they were getting beaten and time was running out, Luke decided to give fate a helping hand, sized up the opposition, selected one of them and gave him a wallop. An all-out mêlée ensued, and the match had to be called off. O'Connell's won the re-match.

As the rest of them recollect it, Luke was always a scrapper. Bessie, who was born a year before Luke, was more like a twin, she said, and being a good bit taller was usually the key to success in any scrapping matches. This didn't weaken Luke's spirit in any way. Mona, who as the eldest often minded him, said, 'He always had a cut here, an arm in a sling, a bandage on the knee,' and a photograph of Mr Kelly with five of his children – before John, the youngest, was born – makes the point: there is Luke, aged perhaps three, with a huge grin and a huge plaster over his right eye.

Luke was also, Mona said, always curious about life, restless to see the world. 'He was always getting lost. He'd wander off and the next thing you'd hear 'Luke Kelly is missing again' and you'd have to go off looking for him. Once he'd gone all the way to Ballsbridge, which was miles from where we were.' His favoured method of travel around the city was the back of a lorry, courtesy of an unsuspecting driver.

The move to Whitehall in 1953 affected Luke badly. Given the Dublin housing shortage, the Kellys would not have been scheduled for a move from what was modern Corporation accommodation, except that the flat was destroyed by a fire. None other than Alfie Byrne, the Lord Mayor, arrived around to console the distraught family and subsequently found them a house in Glen Cloy Road, which Luke hated. He wept bitterly at his changed circumstances, his sisters said, as he made the long journey to and from St Lawrence O'Toole where he was to finish out his education. 'All of a sudden we had to take buses,' Mona said. 'We'd never had to take buses anywhere before.' The only bonus to the move was that Mrs Kelly decided to invest in a gramophone, whereupon Luke bought his first record – Fats Domino's 'Blueberry Hill.'

Like his brothers and sisters, Luke left school at thirteen. Neither intelligence nor scholarship made any difference at that time to an outlook that was determined before a child was born. A surviving bit of evidence from St Laurence O'Toole's – the school report for the 1951 summer term – gives some indication of the kind of student he was: 'very good' at religion, homework, punctuality, and general conduct; arithmetic, 100%, Irish 93%, reading, 85% and English, 80%.

His first job was as a messenger for an electrical goods firm, which, he said candidly in an interview in 1971, he hated: 'I felt it was degrading to be a messenger...Later I was a van assistant for Mitchells, the wine merchants. I remember having to carry a crate of bottles across the Lansdowne Road pitch during a schools rugby match and wishing the ground would swallow me, I was so embarrassed, and felt, again, it was degrading.' The interviewer asked him whether he envied more affluent children, and Luke replied, 'Oh, no, I pitied them. I'd see other kids my own age, all togged up and still having to go to school, while I was free and earning a few bob. I'd feel sorry for them.'

After that he followed the family into Jacobs for a brief spell. At the time he was playing for Home Farm and got a tentative offer to try his hand at the paint trade. Luke left Jacobs and lasted long enough at the painting to do a job at Áras an Uachtaráin. The number of other jobs listed in various reports of his early life include dock work, building work, furniture removal, drain digging and odd-jobbing at Unidare in Finglas, where one of his workmates was Dickie Rock. As his younger brother Jimmy said, 'Luke always said he had more jobs than Ho Chi Min.'

It was the mid-'50s, a period of, if anything, even more concentrated poverty and also the beginnings of a new anger in Dublin. The people had managed to elect an unemployed man, Jack Murphy, to the Dáil. At almost the same time, of course, the bishops ran a campaign to ensure that the Dublin people wouldn't elect 'Red' O'Riordan – Michael O'Riordan, the general secretary of the Irish Communist Party – not that there was any such prospect, as Mick would cheerfully acknowledge. A great hysteria was whipped up against the Corkman who was active as a trade unionist and busman in Dublin. No surprise that when Luke Kelly was at the height of fame in the '60s, he sang at an election rally for Mick O'Riordan.

In 1958, Luke Kelly headed for the Isle of Man in search of hotel work. He was seventeen, and for him and the thousands like him who left Ireland to seek some kind of living and a future in Britain at that time, any vision of hope was still a long way off. But many of them fitted readily into an emerging working-class radicalism in the cities of Britain, and Luke brought with him a sense of Dublin's history, culture and music that needed only awakening to set him on course for life.

CHAPTER TWO

St Lawrence O'Toole Boys' Choir was an exceptionally good one, renowned in the '40s and '50s in Dublin. When young Luke Kelly applied to join, Brother Cordial turned him away and told him to go home and practice the scales. As Paddy, Mona and Bessie Kelly remember it, Luke was told he was either too loud, or too raucous, or perhaps both. Luke, telling the story against himself years later, said he doubted whether Brother Cordial ever regretted his decision. 'I sang as a twelve-year-old the way I sing now. You can imagine what that sounded like among a group of boy sopranos.'

This remark is echoed in another comment Luke Kelly made in a 1975 taped conversation with Frank Harte, the leading exponent of the unaccompanied song and an expert on Dublin ballads. The two were discussing Michael Moran – better known as Zozimus, the most famous or notorious of Dublin's balladeers – and Frank made the point that Zozimus never expressed himself in the manner customary in Irish rural ballads. 'How could he?' Luke replied. 'He had to bawl at the top of his voice to get over the noise of the traffic relating the details of yesterday's murder, and who was drunk last night and where. He couldn't go around singing in a very gentle, rural voice.'

No more could Luke Kelly, and though he had to leave his city like countless others to make his mark, it was Dublin that made Luke Kelly what he was. He drew his great strength from a heritage that combined fine poetry and doggerel verse, the language of the gentry and the slang of the street. And it has proved a lasting heritage – to this day, no European city compares with Dublin for its ready availability of live music and song in public theatres, concert halls or private house parties.

Grafton Street even in a wet Irish summer is the mecca for Europe's if not the world's itinerant buskers. The 'music makers, the dreamers of dreams' are alive and well in Dublin.

The Irish fascination with music goes back a long time. In the 12th-century Cambrensis Giraldus commented on his travels here that the Irish were not only poorly instructed in the rudiments of the faith but a 'filthy people wallowing in vice'; yet 'in the cultivation of instrumental music I consider the proficiency of this people to be worthy of commendation, and in this their skill is beyond all comparison beyond that of any nation I have seen.' Singing was particularly bound up with the custom of story-telling, and it is the tales told in songs, of passion, pain, hope, humour and history, that spurred Frank Harte's interest. That custom has never died out. Frank – whose wry, lilting voice is as unique in its way as Luke's was in his – says in his introduction to *Songs of Dublin*: 'We in this country have been spared the sacredness of revival due to the fact that the tradition of singing songs has never died, and with the number of songs and singers about today, it is unlikely that it will for some time to come.'

In his view, there are some distinct characteristics to Irish singing, one of which is the emphasis on the solo performance. 'Choruses are alien to the Irish tradition,' he told me. 'I don't think I've three songs in my repertoire with choruses – "The Spanish Lady" is one of them. In all our songs, there isn't a chorus in the bunch. And there were never choirs. We were not like the Welsh; we never sang together.' He believes the development of the chorus brought songs out of their original context, where people sat and sang in turn to each other. 'The singer never sang on speculation,' he said. 'He wasn't looking for an audience. He already had his audience, the six people who were sitting in front of him. And he never had to wonder whether they'd appreciate his songs. He never took a chance. He knew everyone he was singing for. 'Thus if a singer opened up with "Come all ye trueborn Irishmen", it was a nationalist audience, and if another sang out "Ye Protestant heroes of Ireland" he knew where he was singing. There was never any speculating for approval; you had it set up before you started at all. '

Frank has also always argued that Dublin songs are an integral part of Irish traditional music, but that it took the Behans, Brendan and Dominic, followed by Luke, to make them acceptable. Before Brendan Behan put the songs on stage, "Molly Malone" and "The Spanish Lady" were the only songs from the capital of which the public was aware, 'sung mainly by the Radio Eireann singers and the girls with the harps in much the same manner as "Danny Boy" is sung,' he said.

'Brendan Behan had a huge effect, because he was the first one who shouted out with a Dublin accent and he didn't give a damn. There was no attempt to add refinement, or corruption if you wish, of the basic Dublin accent. I think the effect of *The Quare Fellow* was huge, because again, he was one of our own. He wasn't from Synge...O'Casey hadn't got the Dublin thing. He had it in his plays, but he didn't have it in his music. He went back to music hall. Whereas Brendan went straight at it, unaccompanied. "The Old Triangle" came out as a revelation. Here was a Dublin song – and remember, at the time you had a great sacred approach to Ireland and to the Irish. We had only come out of the Troubles, and we were trying to portray ourselves as a very nice class of person...then Behan comes along, and then Luke comes along, and shatters the whole damned thing.'

Behan also asserted something of major importance when he spoke and sang, in an unmistakable Dublin accent, in the Irish language. By and large, both the language and the music that were part of the rural tradition had a bad name with Dubliners when I was growing up, and this was almost entirely due to the class of people who had formally and ostentatiously embraced

Irish culture generally, and in my view sought to hijack the music with the language. Myles na gCopaleen satirised the type perfectly in *An Béal Bocht,* where the gaelgóirí – or gaelborri – cast a particularly pompous shadow over the landscape; Brendan Behan did the same in *The Hostage,* where you have the 'Monsewer' wandering earnestly around a brothel, wearing his kilts and playing his bagpipes.

For many years there was an elitism about the Irish language, music, customs and folklore which was associated with civil servants and 'gaelgóirí'. This meant that whatever cultural activity might be on offer was the preserve of a small group of people, a very particular segment of Irish society, and not a very attractive one at that. I must stress that there were honourable exceptions to this pattern, of course, notably in Radio Éireann, which was an important means of raising people's awareness. Those who did have a love for ballads and folklore were well served just by tuning into Seán Mac Réamoinn's *The Ballad Makers Saturday Night,* and later on, *A Job of Journeywork* and *Ceolta Tíre* with Ciarán Mac Mathúna. These programmes, along with Céilí House, still later, were the valiant and excellent work of producers dedicated to bringing into Irish homes the best of the traditional culture, building on the folklore and stories that we had learned a bit about from our parents.

But generally there was little to appeal to ordinary Dubliners. We had, for instance, Sunday-night céilís in the city in those years, but the organisers often made it extremely difficult for anyone to enjoy themselves. The dances tended to be complicated and uncomfortable, requiring dancers to stand up on their toes like elves to execute the steps 'properly'. There was great hostility to anything as barbaric as a Clare set that might risk physical contact between the sexes. Irish dancing was considered a highly respectable exercise, all about putting the hand up and keeping a distance between partners, and tripping through intricate footwork while keeping up with the thump, thump of the staccato music. Much of the music tended to be less than inspiring. A lot of the céilí bands belted out the tunes with a heavy reliance on piano, accordion and drums. And singing wasn't a feature – ballads and *sean nós* were a totally separate enterprise. Céilís were for sprightly dancing and physical exercise. The only time a song would be heard was during the break. I blame this period for the many awful examples of the cross-over from Irish ballads to some of the worst and most sentimental country-and-western songs that dominated dance halls for many years. Luckily, we were rescued by the rise of the showbands, which brought a real professionalism and a better quality of entertainment to the social circuit.

Luke Kelly never spoke in interviews about any exposure to Irish traditional music in his young days in Dublin. But it is not really surprising to learn despite Luke's reticence – whether due to reserve or because he considered the experience of negligible significance – that as a teenager he was an enthusiastic participant in the céilí dancing which was organised in Seville Place as an ancillary activity of the St Lawrence O'Toole Pipe Band. He went with his sister, Mona, who is a set dancer to this day, and started Irish dancing lessons at twelve. 'I had to beg the sixpence for the lessons, and I got it and went right in with the babies and learned my steps and didn't mind a bit,' she said cheerfully. Between 1953 and 1958, Mona and Luke were also involved in an organisation called the Marian Arts Society, which was founded in Mountjoy Square and had a branch in Seville Place. The rest of the family gave them some slagging for their interest – 'We were the squares,' Mona said – but they stuck with it although it meant taking the Number 20 bus in from Whitehall to the old neighbourhood. Luke also loved the square-dancing which the society arranged on Saturday nights, though that was possibly even 'squarer' than céilí dancing.

What is certainly of interest, given Luke's later fondness for the theatre, was that the society's main activity was putting on plays in the Oriel Hall. Among those who began his career in the Oriel was young Jim Sheridan, who was of course from the same north-inner-city area. Luke's first stage part came about in the best of Hollywood style, when one of the actors in a comedy called *Meet The Family* fell sick, and Luke, who had the job of prompter, stepped into the breach. Mona remembers that Luke later organised a black-and-white minstrel number with a line of boys strutting out before the footlights singing 'Swanee' in Al Jolson manner.

This was in keeping with the popular culture of Dublin in the '50s – imports overlaid on ancient forms of expressions. And ancient habits as well, such as solo singing sessions at hoolies or family get-togethers. Luke's brothers and sisters say that long before they had a radio, they had nightly sessions initiated by their father. 'We had to make our own entertainment in those days,' Paddy said. 'I remember well that we'd get around the fire, with my da taking centre-stage in his armchair. It was no more or less than a family way of enjoying ourselves. He knew all the songs and would sing them and then teach them to us. My mother's family were all singers, too, and we always sang at family get-togethers.'

Luke's father sang black spirituals and old favourites and music hall numbers – 'The Spaniard That Blighted My Life' and 'Ragtime Cowboy Joe' and 'She Said She Couldn't Swim' and 'Old Black Joe', as well as some John McCormack specialties. Luke's sisters remember Luke requesting 'Oft In The Stilly Night'. On Christmas mornings, when the Kellys visited their cousins, the Byrnes on Marlborough Street, Paddy said, 'It was like a cabaret. We were all able to do a bit; but never in those days in my wildest dreams did I imagine that Luke could develop into anything like he did.'

Luke may have had more insight into his future.

When they moved to Whitehall, the Kellys went on Sunday nights to the assembly hall in the parish, where there were frequent talent competitions. 'I entered for one and I think I came second – you'd sing Frank Sinatra and Perry Como, that kind of thing,' Paddy said. Luke – who, Paddy said 'was never backward about going forward' – entered too, and Jimmy remembers one memorable occasion when his contribution was a passable Pat Boone rendition of 'Love Letters in the Sand'. Jimmy Kelly, no mean singer himself by any standard, couldn't muster the nerve to put himself forward, but Luke would always have a go. 'He kind of always fancied his chances, fancied that he was a bit of a singer,' Jimmy said. His model was Frank Sinatra, and Jimmy also remembered that Luke would regularly slip away to go home and listen to Frank Sinatra's Sunday night half-hour on Radio Luxembourg and then return to the festivities in the hall.

He also preferred quality professional jazz, which even then marked him out from most devotees of the Top 20, but like almost everyone else, Luke's musical tastes were dominated by America. Our entertainers were straight from the celluloid, going back to Al Jolson – a great favourite in Dublin and frequently parodied at fancy dress and Hallowe'en parties – because the centres of entertainment for most Dubliners were the local cinemas . There was a proliferation of them – the Tivo, the Strand, the Phoenix, the Mero – where the adults queued up on a Sunday night and we could get in for fourpence for the children's mad rush on Saturday afternoon. There were other models much admired, such as Paul Robeson, and still others when the recording industry took on a life of its own, shaking us up with Teresa Brewer, whose 'Music, Music , Music' earned the distinction of a Radio Éireann ban or Bill Haley and his Comets and later Elvis. There was live theatrical entertainment, but little of it reflected Dublin's unique character, apart from the pantos at Christmas time, or the likes of Harry Brogan on stage in the Abbey. In general, however, the Abbey failed to generate a strong identification with the Dublin of that era and did little to inspire Dublin audiences.

As for living music, our public expression of harmony and melody seemed to revolve around bands – pipe bands, brass and reed bands and the Boys' Brigade bands who practiced in basements and paraded to mass on a Sunday morning, who turned up for every boy scout or public event or religious occasion at the local church. There was a great demand for marching bands in particular on St Patrick's Day, and but for the bands, many young people wouldn't have had any musical training. Personal music lessons were a luxury few Dublin working-class families could afford and it was in this band-world that many musicians who played commercially in showbands and jazz groups – and, indeed, eventually in traditional music groups when they finally came into their own a decade later – had their early grounding in music.

This was the musical background Luke grew up in; yet thirty years on, after his death in 1984, Elgy Gillespie, a former *Irish Times* journalist, said he was 'a Dublin street singer in the old street singing tradition, and he was in the purest of senses the real thing. He was young when ballad singing was being taken in off the streets and dusted off for the small club circuits; and then later popularised for stadiums and concert halls and theatres…he died in time to miss the final extinction of pure, authentic Dublin ballad-singing delivered in its rawest and most unsentimental vein.' And though I'm not sure I agree with her verdict on the passing of the genre or the issue of purity, I do agree with her description of Luke. He was the genuine article. But while no doubt he had it in his bones, he could only discover what he knew by instinct when he left us, for Dublin's own tradition of street music was no more held in regard than Irish traditional music was.

I realise now that I was exceptionally lucky in that we

lived directly across the road from two public houses – Fogarty's and O'Neill's of Cornmarket Street (long since demolished) – when I was growing up. Because they were side by side, they were a great patch for street entertainers anxious to make a few bob. But what was significant was that they rarely got inside the public house door. The singers gave us their songs, the musicians plied their instruments and at a given moment they would be allowed in to collect what was possible; otherwise they simply waited long enough for the publican to come out and make a contribution, when they would shift on to another location.

This was a straightforward reflection on the status of the ballad singers and travelling musicians. Publicans certainly didn't see any commercial potential in it, and it was only at great outdoor gatherings – annual commemorations of Wolfe Tone at Bodenstown, for instance, or race meetings – that you would see the balladeers doing well, usually selling penny ballad sheets as well as giving their own performances. Their music was in general not considered appropriate urban entertainment.

Sometimes, of course, the music of these buskers was dreadful but often both singers and instrumentalists were talented and skilled. Before the age of the guitar the string instrument in Dublin was the banjo, or banjo-mandolin, a difficult one to master. Small melodeons and concertinas were commonplace but the harp was rare until the sisters in Sion Hill produced their crop of singing female harpists. There were always fiddles – never violins – and mouth organs, not harmonicas. The accordion was known as 'the box'.

Then there were the 'pipes', a term that in other countries generally means the Scottish war pipes but in Ireland referred to the uileann pipes. These have been a major influence on the sound of Irish music because of their evocative tone, which is very close to the human voice. Leo Rowsome, the great exponent of the uileann pipes, who taught music in the Pipers' Club in Thomas

Street, elevated the status of this instrument. My first experience of the pipes was on the kerb outside the pubs across from our house, where a piper stood enthusiastically creating music I found extraordinary for its strange, eerie wildness.

The particular musician I heard that day, I've learned subsequently, may very well have been Johnny Doran, the traveller. There was a community of travellers living in caravans in the area, and considering the ugly conflict between settled communities and travellers over the last few decades, it's noteworthy how close the travellers then were to the working-class families in the area. When I was making my First Communion the local people collected money for clothes for the young travelling children who were making their Communion with us, and if some of the clothes ended up in the pawn before the great day was over, that was the common lot, too.

Several of the travellers' families were very musical and had songs and instrumental skills handed down over generations – the Fureys, who lived beyond our back wall in Cook Street, being the perfect example. The Fureys made musical instruments, repaired caravans and did extraordinarily good art work, as well as practising and playing music non-stop.

So while all this survived, it was under the surface of a city in the '50s which didn't pay a lot of heed to the traditions. And indeed, those interested in Irish culture and literature tended not to rate the tradition of the city very highly. Even those interested in Irish football and sporting culture tended to think of the Dublin people as 'jackeens', products of the Pale, the people of the early conquest. It was there through the children's street games, rhymes, verses that were passed on from one generation to the next, the vocal music that celebrated city life in its lofty and squalid aspects.

Prompted by Frank Harte in that taped conversation to recall something from his own childhood, Luke sang just such a tune:

Down in Bambow Lane
There is a big fat woman
And if you want to know her name
You have to pay a shillin'.

Sailors one and ten;
Soldiers two and a penny;
Big fat men, two pound ten;
Little kids a penny...

He never could find out where Bambow Lane was, he
said, though he presumed it was a nickname for some
street – no doubt a thoroughfare that must have been
well-known in its day. And almost absently, he then
remembered another catch-cry from the streets around
the Five Lamps: 'A-hall, a-hall, the cow shit in the
market,' which was the signal in what he said was 'a
very rough game indeed. You were dispatched to all
sorts of areas, like: "You go to No 3 balcony in Lawrence
O'Toole's", and of course you put your enemies at the
very top so there no hope of them getting back on time.'
When the 'a-hall, a-hall' was sounded, everyone ran
back. 'You had fellows jumping off balconies and
everything to get back. Last in was given a sentence. You
chose your own punishment, fire or water. If you chose
fire, you were battered black and blue. If you chose
water, I needn't tell you what happened. But the great
thing about it was that you were the next judge, so you
could always get your own back immediately.'

In the Liberties and elsewhere we played 'relievie-o',
that elaborate version of hide-and-seek, where the cry
was 'all-in, all-in, the game's broke up". A characteristic
of those street games was that most of them had their
own chants or songs. The children of Luke's generation
grew up knowing that everything had its incantations,
the ball games, the girls' skipping games, the sports
matches and the running games – 'See the robbers
passing by' and 'If I had a golden ball' and 'At the dirty

end of Dirty Lane lived a dirty cobbler, Dick McClane'. Some of them featured prominently in Behan's plays, or were immortalised by The Dubliners. 'There was an old woman who lived in the woods', sung so caustically and authentically by Ronnie Drew, is one of those on a 1959 collection which Dominic Behan put together with Ewan MacColl, *Streets of Songs: Childhood Memories of city streets from Glasgow, Salford and Dublin*. He notes that this version can be traced to the ballad 'The Cruel Mother'.

Local history and folk rhymes in Dublin expressed the experience of city life. This point has been particularly demonstrated in the superb collections of Irish street songs by Colm Ó Lochlainn, and is evident in works dating back to Zozimus, whom Luke described as 'a musical newspaper man'. A street singer and beggarman, he was born in Faddle Alley beside Black Pits in the Liberties of Dublin in 1794, and he was blind from the age of two weeks. He died in 1846 in 15 Patrick Street, beside the cathedral made famous by Swift. The many songs attributed to or associated with Zozimus display a particularly clever turn of phrase and a sarcasm, wit and classical education. *The Finding of Moses*, one of the best-known, is an excellent example. English, imposed language of the oppressor is slyly twisted and mocked, the Biblical story is juxtaposed on the more ordinary plight of a girl who has a baby she hasn't quite planned a home for, and the whole absurd package is wrapped up in masterfully deft metre and rhyming:

In Egypt's fair land, contagious to the Nile
Old Pharoah's daughter went down to bathe in style

In its best forms, the Dublin ballad makes elegant use of all forms of vulgarity – bog Latin, Gaelic, the Queen's English – and sends up formal style with a solemn face. Sweet Ringsend becomes 'the gem that sparkles on the Dodder' and Johnny Doyle stands attired in 'gorgeous raiment'. Mrs McGrath denounces all foreign wars and vows 'by herrings, I'll make them rue the time that take the legs from a child of mine'. Up in the zoological gardens, they have 'hemales and shemales of every hue'. The characters are strong – Dicey Reilly is the heart of the rowl, and Tim Finnegan doesn't rise faintly but roaring 'Thundering jaysus, did yez think I was dead?' These are songs that vividly describe the underbelly of Dublin life, what life was like below stairs, in tenements, on the streets. City songwriters told city stories: canal songs about the barges, sailors' songs from Ringsend, songs about the human conditions of love, hate and war which are punctuated with street names and street slang. There is not much scope for delicacy, but a strong sense of Dubliners' irreverence for their 'betters'. Romance is simple. Beautiful maidens became 'mots' or possibly were elevated to 'one of the rare old stock', Buckshot Forster 'took a girl and lost her in the Furry Glen.'

Many of the best songs are political. We absorbed rather than took conscious notice of the fact that as inner-city Dubliners we were heirs to a great link with the past – as well as a locked hall door, for instance, my family enjoyed a backyard wall that was no less than a thousand years old, built originally to mark the city boundaries as they then were in the Liberties. Just a few doors down was Napper Tandy's house, referred to in the old Dublin song 'The Spanish Lady'. Our experience of life was hard, but it was also remarkably rich, and that too is in the songs. A great favourite of mine is the ballad 'Ye Men of Sweet Liberties', which still evokes the fierce resentment against the infamous Act of Union in 1801 which abolished the Irish Parliament. The air and the turn of phrase, reflect an idiom very common in the Liberties and require a particular use of English to fit the rhyme. The song also contains elements of the old town criers with their 'Hear ye, hear ye'...

36

On ye does your Zozimus call
To sustain every shuttle and loom
Bring your silks and your satins and tweeds
And your tabarets all in their prime
Oh, bring them forth perfect with speed
As you did in your parliament's time...

James Clarence Mangan, who was born in Fishamble
Street in 1803 and died, spent and destitute, of famine
fever in 1849, left a large number of literary works and
ballads. All the revolutionary movements of Irish history
– the United Irishmen, Michael Dwyer, the Fenians –
were commemorated in Dublin songs. So, of course, was
Parnell remembered in the Dublin folk tradition, not to
mention the bawdy activities of the British army – the
Dublin Fusiliers, the members of Dublin's various
garrisons and their associations with women around the
Phoenix Park or up at the Wellington monument, better-
known to Dubliners as the 'Mollymount'; on up to that
most vigorous and funniest, 'Monto', sung by Luke with
great gusto. Among the many who contributed to this
particular vein of Dublin's music was Peadar Kearney, an
uncle of Behan's, who gave us a number of other songs
besides the national anthem, including the Dublin song
of the 1916 insurrection, 'A Row in The Town' and, of
course, 'Down by the Liffey Side'.

Dublin's story is traced in those ballads, sometimes in
a very distorted and less than objective fashion. But the
songs do give the flavour of times past, the pride and
aspirations of the people, the forceful way they adapted
the English language to give vent to their own
viewpoints. Here was the repository of the national
spirit, the refusal of Croppies to lie down.

And here was a very distinctive style. In his discussion
with Luke, Frank Harte expanded on the point that a
Dublin song is as valid as any song from Connemara,
adding: 'But it's completely different. The Dublin man is
not going to say 'One evening fair as Flora bright her

radiant smiles displayed.' He's going to say 'I met me mot the other morning.' He's never going to get involved in the sentiment that the rural expression can, in the ballad...but the Dublin song is still part of the tradition.'

Luke agreed, but added: 'It's a bastard product. The melodies are the old melodies, but the words are music hall, street calls, a combination of all these things. If you sing real Dublin songs to a real Dublin audience, they can't help but cry at their own wit and their own style. But it's going to be hard for somebody from Connemara to get the nuances of a Dublin song. It's a very localised thing. But the fiddle-playing of Sligo is not the same as the fiddle-playing from Kerry.'

The appreciation of his city's wit and style, whether full of sarcasm or sadness or raw pain, was what came through in Luke's hard-edged delivery. In 1967 he said in an interview that he had no proprietary interest in the Dublin street ballads except to wish they were sung properly: 'When Ronnie Drew, with that ridiculous voice of his, sang 'The Butcher Boy' I liked it for the first time. It's not a Dublin ballad , but it's been adapted to Dublin and it's usually sung by girls in a sugary and meaningless way. Ronnie is hard and unsentimental, which is the way Dublin songs are – hard, monosyllabic, edgy. He mentioned 'Down by the Liffey side' – that line about fish and chips – 'Oh, John, come on for a one and one' – is profound. It's the apotheosis of their walk through the city; it's fundamental and human, all this fellow and his mot can afford. 'Dicey Reilly' is one of the most poignant songs, about a woman who lived and probably lived without respect, but is as much a part of this city as Juno.'

But it was Luke's singing of 'The Old Triangle', Behan's sardonic song of Mountjoy Jail from *The Quare Fellow*, and of a very different Dublin song, Kavanagh's 'Raglan Road', that brought Dublin alive again for many Dubliners. 'Raglan Road' can be sung in a manner so maudlin as to make it almost unbearable, but that clearly wasn't the way Patrick Kavanagh wanted it sung. Luke told the following story in an interview in 1980: 'I was sitting in a pub in Dublin, The Bailey, and as you know in the old days – it's changed a bit now – it was known as a literary pub, an artistic pub. I happened to be sitting there in the same company with Patrick Kavanagh and one or two other poets, and someone asked him to recite a poem, which he did, and then someone asked me to sing a song which I did. Being in the presence of the great man I was very nervous. Then he leaned over to me and said in that sepulchral voice of his – he could hardly get his voice out, he was very old …it was just the year before he died – and he said 'You should sing my song,' and I said 'What's that, Mr Kavanagh?' and he said 'Raglan Road'. So he gave me permission. I got permission from the man himself.'

Luke put memory and loss and a Dublin bittersweet toughness into the poem:

On Raglan Road on an autumn day I met her first
    and knew
That her dark hair would weave a snare that I
    would one day rue.
I saw the danger, yet I walked along the enchanted
    way
And I said, let grief be a fallen leaf at the dawning
    of the day.

CHAPTER THREE

Oh Mother dear I'm over here
And I'm never coming back;
What keeps me here is the rake of beer,
The ladies and the crack.

Luke was one of those who did come back. But he returned, again and again, to his old stomping grounds in Britain. It was where he was educated, like many others, and for him the musical and political educations were inseparable. 'My interest in folk music grew parallel to my interest in politics,' he said. 'I was a Frank Sinatra fanatic, and liked singing swinging modern jazz – none of the old basic stuff. I got involved in left-wing politics, and the music of the left-wing was romantic and rejuvenating. It was about realism…everyone in England then interested in folk music was singing Woodie Guthrie and his music expressed the political insight I am talking about…'

But when he took the boat over the first time, Luke went, as thousands of others did then and later, merely looking for some sort of job to keep him in digs and leave a few bob over to explore independence for the first time. He and a friend, Andy Hackett, headed first for the Isle of Man, hoping for hotel work, though according to Luke's sister Mona, they were unsuccessful. Certainly by the time Luke turned up at his brother Paddy's digs in Leeds, he was nearly destitute and Paddy dutifully fulfilled the older brother's role and fixed him up with a job. Mine did the same for me when I went to work in London on various occasions. In the 1950s, though, London was not yet the customary destination for Dublin emigrants. At that time Dubliners tended to gravitate toward the British midlands to work on the large industrial sites, either as building workers or factory operatives. A substantial number also joined the British Army, where prospects for the sons of the unskilled of Dublin were generally considered better than life at home on the dole.

Paddy Kelly had been in England a year by the time Luke joined him. He'd left originally to try out for a football team, and then joined a crew in a building firm in Wolverhampton which moved about the midlands. He and his mates got Luke a place in the same digs, and from the start the indications were that Luke was not going to settle into the normal life of the Irish labourer in England. First he was thrown out of the digs. 'Luke always had a ravenous appetite,' Paddy said. 'And what they give you in digs is all right, just about enough but not any more.' Luke came in one night late from the pub and wolfed down what he could find in the landlady's kitchen. He owned up immediately the next day, but the landlady was unwilling to forgive such a gross transgression. Next he demanded more money on the job, which almost brought on a mass sacking of the Irish contingent. 'He was only a junior but he was learning steel-fixing,' Paddy said. 'Being Luke, he didn't ask anybody's advice, of course; he just went into the agent and said he wanted the same wages as the rest who were doing steel-fixing. The next thing we heard this roar from the office...'

Luke was genuinely astonished that his reasonable request met with such an outraged response, which was an instant sacking and a threat to the rest of his compatriots. He then embarked on an odyssey of working life, taking up one job after another. Paddy, visiting him in his new digs, found him one time covered in muck from his job cleaning oil drums, on another occasion dressed in a very smart suit – 'the real classic, gloves, overcoat, a Crombie' – suitable for his latest job, selling vacuum cleaners on commission. Paddy did his best to keep tabs on him, but Luke had a blithe attitude toward this kind of thing. On the night they were to return home for the Christmas holidays, Paddy arranged to meet him early outside the City station in Leeds; with two minutes to go there was no sign of Luke. Paddy raced his way around the station and returned in despair to the train, wondering what he would tell his mother: 'and there he was in his seat, reading away, not a bother on him. I nearly killed him. That was Luke.'

The job selling vacuum cleaners took Luke away from Birmingham, and Paddy lost touch for a few months early in 1960. He eventually got a telephone number for him in Newcastle and phoned Luke to ask him to be best man at his wedding in July. It was two days before the wedding, in the early hours of the morning, when his doorbell rang in Birmingham.'

'I got the shock of my life,' Paddy said. 'I said 'Jesus Christ, who's this?' There was Luke with Johnny Reavey. He had the beard, the sandals, and the banjo. He said, 'You're looking for a best man, aren't you? Well, here I am.'

Reluctantly, Luke finally gave in to Paddy's persuasion that a shave and haircut were essential before his family arrived from Dublin for the wedding. The suit was the next issue, since Luke had long ago dispensed with his salesman's outfit. 'When you get married you always get a new suit, don't you? Well, in the wedding pictures I'm wearing the new suit and Luke is in what was my best suit,' Paddy said. Luke gave the suit to Jimmy to pack and take back with him as soon as the wedding was over, announcing that he had no need for it. 'We were in the train station with the cases, waiting to go back to Dublin, when Johnny Reavey comes tearing along shouting, "Open that thing quick! The rent for the next two weeks is in it!" And sure enough, there was the money in the suit coat pocket,' Jimmy said.

Luke stayed in the Birmingham area after that, and called at Paddy and Breda's occasionally on a Sunday. A visible means of support seemed to be of no consequence to him any longer, and Paddy said he had numerous conversations with him along the lines of the-mother's-worried-sick-about-you and what-the-hell-are-you-doing-with-yourself. But it was clear that Luke had found something extremely important to him and had moved into a completely different stage of development.

In years to come, Luke often described what happened to him in the early months of 1960 as a form of instant conversion. While staying in Newcastle he came across a club run by Louis Killen and Johnny Doohan, which offered different seasons for different musical forms. Luke went during the jazz season, but decided to drop in during the folk season to see what was on offer. 'I was a bit blasé. I was a big jazz fan, you know, Frank Sinatra...the sophisticated bit,' he told Frank Harte 'You remember the bum-freezer Italian suits? And the winklepicker shoes; can you imagine me in stuff like that? But I was. And going up the stairs to this club I heard this chorus booming out, all Englishmen and they were singing in harmony. It was a song I'd heard on the radio, and I think the soundtrack of that was done by Dominic Behan. I had been struck by the song, very impressed by the sentiments and tune. And I heard this marvellous harmonic delivery to an English audience...'

The song was the 'The Old Triangle', the classic from Brendan Behan's *The Quare Fella*, and what struck Luke was not only the marvellous harmony but the fact that an English audience was listening, rapt, to a Dublin song. 'It made a tremendous impression on me...this was a music I could actually sing. I didn't need an instrument, didn't need to be able to play a trumpet to play jazz. This was something I could actually dive into, feet first.' And he immersed himself, soaking up the songs, learning ten or twelve a week. 'I really forgot how to listen to anything else. I just wanted to hear folk songs.'

So at that time did mass audiences in Britain. Ewan MacColl, the man who was the most important force in the folk music revival, a revival that had such strong ideological roots, dates the start of it to a radio series called *Ballads and Blues* which he had scripted several years earlier. Each programme dealt with different themes – war and peace, love, work, city life – and combined American songs and singers such as Ma Rainey and Big Bill Broonzey and British songs, sung by Ewan, Bert Lloyd and Isla Cameron. The object was to show that England, Scotland and Wales had a body of music about the ordinary life of the poor that was just as vigorous and colourful as that of the United States. The series was a huge success. Up to that time, there had been various surges of interest in folk music, largely among students and a small elite, which died away. Now the English and Scots working class began to adopt the music as their own. A considerable amount of work had also been done for the BBC by Seámus Ennis, the north county Dublin piper and folklorist, and Dominic Behan, Brendan's brother.

The other influence that can't be ignored was the relatively short-lived and good-humoured 'skiffle' craze. As Mary Hardy wrote in her memoir of Luke, the period in which he stumbled into the folk music scene was that of 'the great skiffle disaster'. Much as skiffle is derided it afforded young people encouragement to acquire cheap guitars and construct tea-chest basses and for the first time in a very long time they began to play their own music and explore their own music.' As the guitars became commonplace from one end of Britain to the other, so folk clubs were spawned across the country.

The northern cities of England and Scotland – indeed those of Northern Ireland – have always been famous for workers' clubs, where the working class communities gathered to provide their own entertainment, organise their own social activities and keep the price of drink within affordable range. Those clubs remain an important part of the cultural life of industrial cities in Britain, and have made popular live entertainment available to millions of people at modest cost. The new folk clubs of the late '50s and early '60s were largely located upstairs or downstairs in licensed premises, where the musicians and singers drew in their own audiences and developed their individual styles, free from the hubbub of normal pub entertainment. Irish and Scots performers were always in great demand because they conveyed such immediate and authentic tradition and vitality. As with American folk music, much of that music related to protest and struggle against injustice, to workers' lives and the suffering and joy of poor communities, to emigration, prejudice, human rights. The anti-war songs and CND songs were particularly prevalent, sung on the great Aldermaston marches, and the words and music of Guthrie, Pete Seeger and Leadbelly rang throughout Britain, as later did those of Joan Baez and Bob Dylan.

My own experience of London in the late '50s and early '60s was very much of an Irish community whose members stubbornly insisted on seeing themselves as temporary visitors and were reluctant to integrate into the mainstream. We had our own musical centres side-by-side with the new rash of folk clubs. Huge numbers of young Irish workers and Irish musicians packed into the sessions in Irish pubs and dancehalls. Generally, those sessions were much noisier and the audiences less sedate than the appreciative folk club audiences, but they did provide an outlet for emigrant performers looking for regular weekend work. In many cases, just as Captain O'Neill found in Chicago fifty years earlier, the standard of musicianship was higher than it was at home. Ciarán Mac Mathúna discovered this when he visited London to make recordings for Radio Éireann of wonderful musicians – Seámus Ennis, of course; Roger Sherlock, Julia Clifford, Paddy Taylor, Bobby Casey and many other regulars in London's Irish pubs. Another famous duo in those days was Margaret Barry, a ballad singer with a magnificent public house voice, and Michael O'Gorman, who accompanied her on the fiddle in Camden Town sessions. I loved these sessions and spent many nights listening to the music above the bar-room bawling, and always hoped the performers would one day get the recognition they deserved.

Luke found his way on to the folk club circuit by way of the road. With Johnny Reavey, who had a great store of songs, he went busking through the English Lake District. As Luke always told the story, it was Johnny who did the busking and *his* task was to carry the banjo. It was a five-string banjo, and carrying it Luke got interested in strumming.

Johnny taught him the basic licks. He returned to Dublin on a holiday and met Johnny Moynihan, who directed him to O'Donoghue's and suggested that first he should try a fleadh cheoil. At the time, Luke admitted he didn't even know what a fleadh cheoil was but he went to Milltown Malbay to find out. Luke returned with Colm Ó Lochlainn's famous book and a store of new songs, and begin to stand up and sing for the audience in folk clubs instead of just listening.

As for his political development, there is no question that much of that took place in the home of Sean and Mollie Mulready at 210 May Lane in Birmingham. Sean Mulready was an Irish communist and a scholar whom readers of Irish newspapers might recognise more readily as Seán Ó Maolbhríde, which was how he signed himself at the end of the many letters he wrote over the years to the papers on political matters. He was a teacher of English, Irish and mathematics at the technical school in Great Denmark Street in the 1950s, until the *Catholic Standard* conducted a successful campaign against him as a dangerous radical, using his photograph and naming his place of employment – a foolproof method of persecution. Little by little, his hours of work were reduced until he could no longer make ends meet and he was forced to leave the vocational education system. Rosse College on Stephen's Green, unsusceptible to such pressures, hired him, but in 1958 Sean emigrated to a job in a secondary modern school in Birmingham, and his wife and two sons, Seamus and Liam, followed shortly afterward. In Birmingham, Sean's work was as a teacher of English as a second language. 'He brought children of all nationalities to a basic minimum required by the educational authority, so that they could assimilate into the educational system in Britain, and this sometimes brought him in touch with children from Gaeltacht areas of Ireland,' his son Liam told me.

By 1961, Luke, in diligent pursuit of his vocation, had joined the Clarion Choir, which had connections with the co-operative movement. Katherine Thompson, who was married to George Thompson, professor of Greek at Birmingham University, was a member of the choir, as was Mollie. They befriended Luke. He joined the Mulready household in Easter of 1961, after he was ejected from digs by yet another landlady. This time it was not for the crime of eating too much, but singing too much; Luke practised his trade at home, and his Dublin-born landlady stormed into his room while he was recording himself. Inevitably, Luke recorded her bawling him out and young Liam Mulready later drew great amusement from playing this back to everyone he met.

Sean was an active member of the British Communist Party at that time – he was to resign some years later. The Mulready home was open to everyone, particularly left-wing radicals and musicians. Here, the Irish political and musical links begin to come full circle. One of Sean Mulready's sisters, Kathleen Moynihan, was a founder member of Comhaltas Ceoiltóirí Éireann in Mullingar. Another sister, May, was married to Máirtín Staunton, the Liverpool man who made his home in Spiddal and made such vagabond fleadh followers as Barney McKenna and myself welcome. Máirtín's sister was married to Festy Conlon, and Máirtín himself was interned in the Curragh with Máirtín Ó Cadhain and, among others, two of my first cousins, Mattie and Christy O'Neill.

Máirtín's successful Irish enterprise in Spiddal was

one of the first to export to the United States the Aran
ganseys the Clancy Brothers had made famous there, and
Seamus remembers that once when Máirtín and May
were visiting the Mulreadys, Luke asked whether
Máirtín, too, was a communist; to which Máirtín replied
promptly, 'No. I'm a tycoon.' On the other side of the
Mulready family was Mollie's brother, Ned Stapleton, a
left-wing republican who'd been jailed in England and
spent much time at the Mulready home. Ned, who was a
member of the Scéim na gCeárdchumann during the
years I was involved with that organisation, was a lovely
flautist. It was Ned who taught Luke that trickiest of all
songs, 'The Rocky Road to Dublin.' It is a slip-jig, and
requires such control that few singers attempt it, and
Barney McKenna paid Luke the highest tribute when he
said 'Most people that sing it, they kind of phrase the
words to suit their own power, their own balance. But
Luke could actually sing it the way it's played on a
fiddle. He could sing it to the rhythm.'

Liam Mulready recalls that it was while he was living
with them that Luke bought his first banjo 'and mastered
two chords, over and over again!' He worked as a
storeman by day, and pursued his interest in music by
night. He also developed a love for golf that he had for
life and would never have acquired in Ireland. Here at
that time the game was associated only with private
clubs for the well-off, but in Birmingham, there was a
municipal golf course conveniently situated at the end of
the Mulreadys' garden. Luke also joined both CND and
the Birmingham Young Communist League during his
eighteen months or so with the Mulreadys, and toyed
with the idea of an academic career. 'He was encouraged
to sing, sing, sing by Mollie and to read, read, read by
Sean,' Seamus said. 'Professor Thompson encouraged
him to study and he took to night classes. The idea was
that if he achieved some grades, George – who had great
contacts in eastern Europe – would be able to secure a
place for him at Prague University.'

The music won the day. Luke's closest friend and colleague at this time was Dave Phillips, the Welsh folk singer, with whom he made a record. He also became heavily involved in the Jug O'Punch folk club run by the famous Ian Campbell, although there was some personal rivalry between the two; Ian's sons, Ali and Robin, made musical history themselves in the late '70s when they launched one of the very first radical modern music groups, UB40.

Luke began to make a name for himself in the folk clubs. Dave Neligan, an Irish Labour Party activist for many years, remembers one such club over a pub in London, which he frequented during the years when he lived in exile. Luke and Dominic Behan, that other great Dubliner, were the main attractions, and as he recollects the evenings were hilarious, the music interspersed with jokes and banter. Luke one night told a story that sent his Irish audience into great laughter, of sitting on the upper deck of a bus and watching a row develop between two young fellows from Northern Ireland and a West Indian bus conductor. The dispute concerned the reluctance of the Irishmen to pay the required fare, but they were eventually faced down by the West Indian, a large and imposing man. When he had taken the money and was descending the stairs, one of the Northerners leaned over the edge of the bus and roared down 'Bloody Orangeman!', a remark that left all non-Irish passengers utterly mystified.

Janie Buchan, the Labour MEP for Glasgow who has become a good friend of mine in the European Parliament, remembers Luke well from Glasgow, where he followed Dominic Behan into many a watering hole. Luke was a great supporter of progressive causes and extremely generous with his talent and his time, she said, whether for fund-raisers for the local céilí band or for CND, anti-war concerts or socialist campaigns.

Interestingly enough, Janie recalls that many of the Glasgow CND songs were actual parodies of both

Orange and green songs. One, modelled on 'Hello, hello we are the Billy Boys' became 'Hello, hello, we are the Eskimos' – after an American admiral described the CND campaigners as ' a bunch of Eskimos'. In Glasgow The Dubliners won the hearts and minds of many ordinary people 'who could identify readily with their songs, repartee and working-class earthiness.'

Máirín Johnston, a true Dub herself, first saw Luke at about that time at one of the weekly ballad sessions of Ewan MacColl and Peggy Seeger's Singers' Club in the Pindar of Wakefield on Gray's Inn Road. On that particular night, Ewan MacColl introduced a 'new and very talented ballad singer from Dublin' and Luke stepped forward with a dazzling smile and his shock of curly red hair. When he started to sing, Máirín said, 'my heart sank with disappointment – not at the singing, but at the song which was "There Were Three Lovely Lasses from Kimmage". It was one of my pet hates and still is. However, his next song was "The Foggy Dew" and to this day, no one has ever sung it better than Luke.'

Years later when she was back in Dublin and Luke was very famous, Máirín was given the task of trying to find Luke to enlist The Dubliners for a concert in the Mansion House to aid the anti-apartheid movement. He was proving impossible to track down, and just as she'd given up Luke contacted her. 'He heard on the grapevine that I wanted him to sing for the concert. Thanks to Luke's co-operation, the concert was a tremendous success. Throughout his singing career Luke displayed this same kind of commitment and solidarity towards oppressed and exploited peoples all over the world. He was the definitive Dubliner,' she said.

But Luke found inventive ways to merge music and politics, to the gratitude of his comrades. Sean Redmond, who was working with the Connolly Association based in London in those days, remembers how he did it: 'While we had a fairly extensive network through Britain, we could never crack Birmingham. In the words of the late Desmond Greaves, "It was the last place God made, and even he gave up and never finished it." Trade union membership was then dominated by the car industry workers, with shift working. So it was very hard to maintain any organisation, but that did not stop us trying. Every so often, we would make a special effort and it was during one such blitzkrieg that I first met Luke.'

By that time Luke had joined the Association and gave a hand with the work, but as Sean says, 'More important, he lent his voice. At week-ends we toured the Irish pubs, selling the *Irish Democrat*. With Luke on board, sales rocketed.

'The drill was quite simple. He would go up to the stage or music stand, sing a few songs, then announce that he was here selling the Connolly Association's paper and he expected everybody to buy one.' Clearly, he'd come a long way in effective sales techniques since his vacuum cleaner days.

Sean continued to meet him every time he ventured into the town that God gave up on and also remembers running into him once in London, at King's Cross tube station. 'He had a very earnest look about him and wasn't hanging about for any chat...he explained that he was heading for the Pindar of Wakefield pub. Ewan MacColl was putting a show together and Luke was on his way to audition. He was sucessful in gaining a part and toured Britain with the show, which naturally had a political content.'

The Pindar of Wakefield was then the venue of the Singers' Club. It was the successor to the Ballad and Blues Club, which Ewan started in the Princess Louise pub in High Holborn in 1954, featuring as regular singers Seámus Ennis and Bert Lloyd, and it had a reputation that surpassed that of most of the clubs that flourished during those years. By the early 1970s there were 2,500 folk clubs in Britain. At some point shortly before he returned to Dublin, Luke ventured as far as France and tried his luck busking in Paris, where, he remarked tersely, 'I didn't exactly starve.' But he liked the experience, and came home, Mona said, very impressed by the beauty of Chartres Cathedral. Even though he returned to Ireland, O'Donoghue's, the Gate revues and the launch of The Dubliners in 1962, Luke didn't relinquish his objective to return to that circle in the Singers' Club and to take up a serious apprenticeship under Ewan MacColl.

CHAPTER FOUR

When all the world is young, lad,
And all the trees are green;
And every goose a swan, lad,
And every lass a queen;

Then hey for boot and horse, lad,
And round the world away:
Young blood must have its course, lad,
And every dog its day.
('Young and Old', Charles Kingsley)

I came back to Dublin in 1961 and I knew that there
was an incipient folk song revival here. People
were realising that the songs of Ireland could be
sung with a healthiness we hadn't known before.
They could be taken from the drawing-room and
made to come alive again."
(Luke in an interview in *The Irish Times*,
December, 1967)

Perhaps the most unexpected development of the
exuberant '60s was the sudden boom in the ballad
movement in Ireland. Its great strength, and in many
respects the strength that has lasted as a foundation for
generations of Irish music since, was that it was a fusion
of a number of different strands of considerable strength.

There was a growing international new interest in folk
music. Ireland was strongly affected by the American
folk revival that was to culminate in Woodstock in 1969
and the British movement which Luke had been
schooled in. But in Ireland there was a second strand, a
source waiting to be tapped, in the great body of Irish
music. The people discovered that old songs they'd

heard in school and at home – the bit of music they knew something about, the ordinary tunes that hadn't been much admired – were suddenly the right songs to sing. At last we had music everybody could take part in. I think the cornerstone of success was this level of participation – there was a new realisation that we had an art form, an entertainment form, which everyone could instantly be part of and contribute to. It was ours. It felt right and made us feel good. It was a highly democratic movement; not always musically correct, or politically correct either. But it it did have the crucial characteristics of identification – popular expression and ready access.

There was no shortage of sources. We didn't have to use pickaxes and shovels and fishing nets to locate our culture; nor did we have to dig up manuscripts of the last century. The music and songs had survived and been adapted and had immediate relevance. That gave a substance and individual character to what might have otherwise been weak imitiation.

We were also extremely lucky to have, during that period, talented experts who were readily available – the likes of Séamus Ennis, and Seosamh Ó hÉanaí, who was a rich resource for The Dubliners, and Darach Ó Catháin and of course Seán Ó Riada, who broke new territory with his Ceoltóirí Chúlainn. We also had very good ballad collections such as Colm Ó Lochlainn's , the many Walton publications and a variety of other sheets.

Luke, talking in 1975 about the immediate success The Dubliners met with across continental Europe, pointed out that Swedish, German and Dutch audiences saw Ireland as still vibrant musically. 'They saw us as being representative of something that they had lost. Since then we've got Planxty going and the Chieftains going, and they give the real expressions, much more in-depth expressions I would say, of what really is representative. But we actually made the break for them,' he told Frank Harte. And while agreeing that the credit for popularising Irish music went to such groups as the Clancys and The

Dubliners, he said the responsibility for keeping it alive had to go to 'the people who held on to it; the people who played fiddles and kept on playing them, no matter what intrusions the showbands made.' Like the vast majority of Dubliners, he said, his attitude had been that 'it was culchie music' but he had learned that far from being crude, Irish traditional music was in fact ingenious and subtle. 'Joe Heaney's singing may sound to the uninitiated ear maybe a bit crude and a bit hoarse, but Joe Heaney is a marvellously subtle singer. His phrasing, the way he states what he has to state; it's beautiful...'

To those of us who were at the time seeking out traditional music – and were widely regarded for our pains as a bunch of cranks – Seán Ó Riada especially brought a message of changed circumstances. Maire Mhac an tSaoi once defined Irish pleasure in a memorable lecture as drinking porter from a bucket at the gable end of the cottage on a windy night, which is more or less how traditional musicians saw themselves. Those who aspired to make a living from it expected to play for pennies, or as poor Raftery said long ago, 'playing music to empty pockets', the lot of Irish musicians since the harpers and the pipers lost their places in the big houses of Ireland. When they were lucky they played for porter but more often they played for personal enjoyment. Seán Ó Riada opened the door again and musicians no longer had to think of themselves in terms only of the back kitchen or the back room of the pub.

The small intimate Dublin clubs where the traditional musicians had been meeting for years began to pick up new custom. We had the Pipers Club; the excellent club in Church Street called 'The Fiddlers' Club' which was really St Mary's Music Club; the Clareman's Club in Bridge Street where we found we could dance sets to our hearts' content without interference from any straight-laced 'gaelgóiri' who for years had rejected Clare sets as being too undignified.

And most important, there was what turned out to be an Irish solution to the Irish problem of the era, the fleadh cheoils. These festivals of music and song were organised by Comhaltas Ceoiltóirí Éireann, the organisation of Irish traditional musicians which has as its objective the promotion of the music in all its forms. The first was held in 1951 in Mullingar, and had an attendance of about 1,500; but by the mid-'60s 'the fleadh' was attracting 100,000. They were a powerful force, and a focus for young people who were aching to break through to a better future. Luke was one of those most affected. 'I was coming back here for Christmas and holidays, the usual,' he said, 'and then I began going to the odd fleadh cheoil. And that brought it even more forcibly home to me that there was something back here. Because when I went away in the first place I had no intentions of coming back. But I was re-seduced, if you like.'

The music was assuming new character and a life of its own. It was attracting more followers, entertaining bigger audiences and bringing new vitality into the old musical forms.

Fleadh cheoil were organised formally for musical competitions, concerts and exhibitions, but they had a cumbustive effect in releasing pent-up energy and a sense of enthusiasm and pleasure. The youthful exuberance was not always appreciated by parish priests and bishops, who sounded some alarm at the liberal, lively and Rabelaisian character of these gatherings. The summer fleadh acted like a magnet. It drew young people from across the country into one concentrated hooley in a small rural town, a different place each year. We camped and slept out in any available shelter. I have a vivid memory of putting in a night in the portico of a church where the bells roused me on the hour and half-hour.

The fleadh incited a friendly Irish anarchy. I spent some of the most enjoyable days of my life in Connemara with Barney McKenna, when we went AWOL after a Clare fleadh and travelled up to Spiddal and Ceathrú Rua. There we found Festy Conlon and Paddy Bán Ó Broin and the Staunton family, who gave us a welcome fit for kings although we were both broke and without visible means of support. The welcome for music and crack was prompt and warm, and absolutely in character with the way travelling musicians were treated in earlier times. We had the hospitality of Festy's home and Tim Johnny Folen's shed in the village of Spiddal, and were given great accommodation and the best of everything by Máirtín and May Staunton. Later we heard the best of *sean-nós* singing in Ceathrú Rua from Tomas MacEoin, Peadar Tommy and Máire Ní Dhonnchadh, and were taken in by Bartley Shéamus Ó Loidean agus a bhean at An Rinn. At the time, Tigh Chatháin, run by Pádraig Ó Catháin, himself a fine *sean-nós* singer and musician, was a great venue for Connemara box players and singers.

But sleep was only a necessity when exhaustion set in, and the fleadhs saw people singing and dancing in the streets most of the night, reacting joyfully to an ancient and sometimes savage music that penetrated the solar plexus as well as stimulating the folk memory. For some it was a first wonderful defiance of convention, breaking down decades of Puritan constraint and respectable moralising. It was, as Christy Moore sang in 'Lisdoonvarna', a confluence of 'amhráns, bodhráns and amadháns' or an updated variation on 'The Galway Races' theme, belted out so vigorously by Luke: 'There was half a million people there of all denominations, The Catholic, the Protestant, the Jew and Presbyterian. There was yet no animosity no matter what persuasion/ But sportsman hospitality inducing fresh acquaintance! Whack fol-the-dol for the diddley-diddle-day...'

They came in their droves, fellows with their mots often sharing a sleeping bag, washing in the river and dancing with other people's wives. The musicians who had been keeping their talents for small intimate gatherings of the converted suddenly found themselves with a mass audience. There was also a sudden proliferation of guitars and bodhráns, creating a din that at times prevented musicians from hearing themselves or each other. Thankfully, amplification was a rarity so the dedicated new rhythm section didn't succeed in killing the music altogether; but musicians got a certain satsifaction from the reported reply of one piper – either Willie Clancy or Seámus Ennis – to a bodhrán enthusiast who asked whether it was best to play with the hand or a stick: 'Neither. With a knife.' Seán Ó Riada had popularised the bodhrán to such an extent that no goat was safe and every tone-deaf fleadh reveller had a lethal weapon to batter around Ireland.

Inevitably the audience wanted to be part of the action and the singing became an integral part of the fleadh, in impromptu sessions in pubs and in the open streets where performers would huddle together wherever they met. Singers, songwriters, instrumentalists from city and town and farms met and got on famously with 'Fine Girl You Are' or 'Seven Drunken Nights'. The stopper was off the bottle and the genie of the people's music was out. The crack was mighty; young blood was having its course and no one was going to stop it.

Not everyone was pleased. Breandán Breathnach, the finest collector of genuine traditional music material, was to write ruefully in *Ceol*, his Irish music journal, about the evolution of Comhaltas Ceoltóirí Éireann: 'A local branch of this association has been permitted to participate in organising a ballad competition for groups. The ambition of the organisers, we are told, is to make this festival famous throughout Ireland and an annual event in the town's cultural activities. The sponsor was another tobacco company, whose representative informed the audience that ballads and folk music were very much a part of the tourist industry.'

And so it was to be. But there was another strand

which gave a particular character to the ballad movement in Ireland, and that was the rising political consciousness of young people. As we developed a specifically Irish social purpose and political direction, the ballad movement became our own means of expression. There was a long tradition of nationalist songs, tales of woe, heroic resistance and rejection of our conquest. These go back to Thomas Davis and the Young Irelanders, the Fenians and the Invincibles, and continued through the period of the Independence movement, the Civil War and each decade since. Some of these are hardly worthy of preservation, but others have an inspirational quality and convey a lot of genuine and legitimate feeling about our past. They have often served to record great historic events and bridge the gap between past and present in a unique way.

What was happening now, though, was different. This was a modern political expression both Irish and universal, part of the 'get up and go' mood of the '60s. That isn't to say that everyone involved in 'the ballads' had a particular political focus. But that ebullience and audacity that characterised the music was stimulated by the new popularity of 'protest concerts' for every cause. The annual Connolly Concert in Liberty Hall was a forum for struggle and protest in which Luke and The Dubliners played their part, donating their services generously.

This mood penetrated the mass media and entered into the popular mainstream. Even the financial institutions who made so much money out of entertainment were suddenly obliged to take on board the protest movement – the Bob Dylans, the music of people in the mould of Woody Guthrie, Joan Baez, Ewan MacColl, Pete Seeger. Only in these unique circumstances could a song like 'We Shall Overcome' become universal, applicable to all those suffering, as likely to be heard on the airwaves and in entertainment halls far removed from any particular social upheaval as at a civil rights meeting in

Belfast or a Dublin housing march.

One of the early organisers of ballad sessions was Peggy
Jordan, a Dublin woman whose interest in Irish music
dates back to her childhood. As a pupil in Scoil Bhríd,
Mrs Gavan Duffy's school, her favourite classes were the
singing sessions where the children learned Gaeltacht
songs of every kind. As an adult she joined one of the
liveliest branches of the Gaelic League, Craobh na gCúig
Cúigi, which met in Ely Place and where traditional
music and dancing sessions were free-spirited and not
cursed by the staidness which afflicted so many Gaelic
League sessions. She was also a member of the group
which founded the first An Óige hostel in Blessington,
Co Wicklow, where weekend sessions were often held,
and of the GAA. Not one for purist attitudes, Peggy saw
great potential in the new movement and became a part
of it.

She maintained her interest in traditional music after
her marriage. Tom and Peggy Jordan's home in
Kenilworth Square, one of the most hospitable in Ireland,
became during the '60s an unofficial centre for sessions,
especially after-hours sessions. Despite rearing a large
family, Peggy followed the music whenever she could,
and she was at the Fleadh in Ennis where the Clancy
Brothers made an appearance after their success abroad.
They were a new sight for regular fleadh-goers and had a
dramatic impact on all of us – this family from Carrick-
on-Suir, in their báinín jumpers, bringing a sense of
polished entertainment to some very old worn songs.
There is no doubt that the unexpected and enormous
success of the Clancys fuelled a new professionalism
among Irish musicians and gave a great impetus to the
movement that was emerging; but of course there was
also a lot of uncertainty about this commercial and
obviously well-organised and rehearsed group back from
America. They didn't fit either the old or the new
stereotypes but they were clearly a force to be reckoned

Luke in characteristic style, smoking, drinking and
having crack in London on his return from a tour of
Africa, late 1960s
(Photograph: Seán Geraghty)

The Dubliners performing at a concert in London, late
1960s
(Photograph: Seán Geraghty)

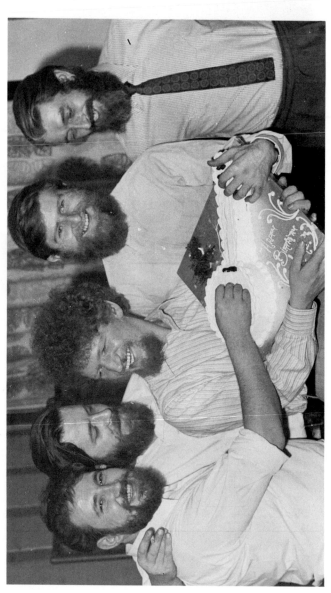

Luke and Barney share the banjo at Luke's birthday celebration in Fairfield Hall, Croydon.
The animated Dubliners are, from left: Barney McKenna, Ciarán Bourke, Luke, John Sheahan, Ronnie Drew

(Photograph: Seán Geraghty)

Deirdre O'Connell and Luke's brother, Jimmy in the
Palace Bar
(Photograph courtesy of Jimmy Kelly)

Luke signing on with London promoter,
Seán Mac Gabhann
(Photograph Seán Geraghty)

The Seventies
The Dubliners (all except John Sheahan) enjoying a pint

'The flautist' — author Des Geraghty

with. They had great stage presence and exuberance and were definitely going places.

The Clancys joined the many other singers and musicians who often arrived at the Jordans' house late on a Friday night and stayed the weekend. It was after one such whopping party that Peggy got a call from Minnie Scott-Lennon of the Abbey Tavern. She wanted Peggy to get the new ballad musicians into the Abbey, and, as Peggy remembers, 'Liam Clancy was staying there and we piled into my Volkswagen and went out to Howth.' Peggy agreed to take on the organising of sessions at the Abbey Tavern.

Dara Ó Lochlainn's version casts a different light on the event: 'My brother Ruan well remembers the proprietress of the Abbey Tavern in Howth, Minnie Scott-Lennon, telling him after a real rave-up Dixieland jazz session that he and his band were fired and that "a real nice crowd of ballad people were taking over – not rowdy like your lot".'

Peggy told Minnie Scott-Lennon at the outset that the place was too small and that she would have to build an annexe. Peggy was right. Her open attitude towards music ensured success: 'There are only two kinds of music, good and bad.' Thus from the start she saw to it that the programme mixed Irish traditional music with folk music from elsewhere – 'We'd even throw in a bit of classical.' From her own extensive guest lists and by word of mouth, Peggy began auditioning for the Abbey Tavern. The auditions were held in her home but pressure was so great that eventually she began to audition by telephone while looking after six children in the background. She put together teams that became famous and drew huge crowds, Jesse Owens and Anne Byrne among them, and frequently got involved in arranging the presentation of the songs.

From that point, the 'ballad movement' as it was known, began to explode in Dublin. There were sessions in the International Bar, the Hollybrook in Clontarf, and the 'Ballads at Midnight' sessions in the old Grafton Cinema on a Saturday night. Peggy and her entourage of singers and musicians often came straight from the Abbey Tavern into Grafton Street, varying the programmes from one venue to the next.

One night the concert programme offered a duo during the first half – Barney McKenna on the banjo and on the spoons, Mary Jordan, who is now one of Ireland's leading environmental activists. They were such a hit with the audience that they gave an encore during the second half, joined by Ronnie Drew with his guitar. 'That's how it started,' Peggy says. As she recalls it, the 'Ronnie Drew Group' (at least in one of its incarnations) was afterwards launched in a restaurant on Lincoln Place which has gone under several names since, but was then called 'the Granada.'

This was the Ireland that Luke came home to in 1962. Peggy remembers Luke with a banjo case full of Communist literature, which fell out when he opened it to take out the banjo. As Luke related it to Frank Harte, he came back from England not knowing anyone except Johnny Moynihan, though he had heard Barney playing, and like many Dubliners by then, he knew Ronnie Drew from his performances in the John Molloy productions at the Gate. Ronnie had begun playing ballads at intervals in the Gate after his return from a three-year sojourn in Spain – where he taught English and worked as an extra in *Lawrence of Arabia*, among other things – and had also developed a great interest in flamenco guitar.

But it was some time before anything as cohesive as a group evolved. A collection of musicians gathered around and Luke was often but not always among them. Ronnie Drew was a stable centre for this band of troubadours who performed, off and on, at various sessions. Peggy's memories of those days are of hectic activity: 'I would bathe my two youngest and get them to bed and then drive out to collect the musicians, getting them to tune up in the car. I was always after them, insisting that they had to be in tune and they had to be on time – had to be professional.'

None of this crowd had much notion of the business side of the performance arts. Their priorities were elsewhere. It was a job to keep them on the rails, and Peggy routinely sent people home for clean shirts and socks and then moved heaven and earth to get them to their gigs on time. On the night Ronnie and the others were to meet the press at a formal reception, the musicians decided to have a preliminary drink at O'Donoghue's. 'Next thing,' Peggy said, ' I get a phone call to say they wouldn't be going to the reception; they'd got a lift to Puck Fair.' Peggy was in the middle of putting the dinner on the table. As luck would have it, Liam Clancy, by then highly successful, was again staying in the Jordans' home and she pressed him to drive with her down to O'Donoghue's. 'They couldn't see what the fuss was about. They said 'It's only a press reception; you just tell them about us.' Liam Clancy, whom Peggy remembers was still half-asleep, his hair tousled, looked at them mildly and said 'Listen, lads; even the great Clancys have to go to their own press receptions.'

Various venues have been identified as the historic locale of the first actual coming-together of The Dubliners. All of them identify licensed premises. Dara Ó Lochlainn says that the group came together first at the Pembroke Bar round the corner from O'Donoghue's: 'Riotous sessions took place at the drop of a hat or the rise of a pint.' Hayden Murphy, in his memoir of Luke, recalls that he first met Ronnie Drew in the International Hotel on Wicklow Street.

But in fact, whatever else, they also performed. O'Donoghue's was undoubtedly home base, even before The Dubliners were formed, even before it became a rehearsal centre. Con Houlihan, reminiscing about Luke after his death, wrote in the *Evening Press*, 'I cannot put a date on our first meeting – but it was so long ago you could get a fine counter lunch for three shillings and sixpence in O'Donoghue's of Merrion Row. It was then anything but a singing pub. I frequented it because I was involved with the Department of Education around the corner – Luke used to come to meet Ronnie Drew who had a flat nearby.

'In that far-off era ballad singers were people you saw at fairs or football matches. Luke had a vague romantic notion that some day he might be a professional singer but I doubt if he or I believed it. A few years later came the flood of what is loosely termed folk music, probably precipitated by the civil rights movement in the USA. It would be less than accurate to say that Luke caught the tide; it was rather that the tide caught him...'

O'Donoghue's became a musical headquarters, especially for those interested in singing, after John Molloy, who lived around the corner, asked the proprietor, Paddy O'Donoghue, if some of the musicians could use his backroom to practise in when it was closed to trade. Soon musicians around Dublin started to gravitate to O'Donoghue's back room and stay there from morning to night. One of these was Ciarán Bourke, then studying agriculture at University College, Dublin. Those of us who were working came at lunch hours, to get in a few tunes and a few pints. As I remember it, there were often only a few who forced themselves reluctantly to get back to work.

Like the others, Luke, who was still without a job, was fed by Maureen O'Donoghue when times were hard. Always independent, he continued to pursue his own interest in songs with political content. The journalist and folk columnist Joe Kennedy recalled in an article: 'Some time before Jack Kennedy's assassination, he showed me one night in O'Donoghue's some songs written by a person called Bob Dylan. 'His real name is Zimmerman,' said Luke, 'and you have to read this stuff.' It was in an American magazine called *Sing Out*, then unavailable here. The songs were of social issues, of course, and

American, and there was one called "Blowin' in the Wind" which Luke said would be popular, though he was characteristically sceptical enough to wonder if Dylan had written it at all.'

The turning point for what was still The Ronnie Drew Group came with a concert John Molloy organised in the old Royal Hibernian Hotel which Luke said was 'the first organised ballad session as such, with people paying in.' It was a sensational success, so much so that John decided on a large-scale production in the Gate, called *A Ballad Tour of Ireland*. Luke was part of the group which played ballads from different counties, interspersed with local tales from John, using his gift for accents and mimicry to advantage. The show was an extraordinary success and made the group that wasn't actually a group seem so in the eyes of Dublin's people.

It was also, according to Luke's brother, Paddy, the event that explained to his family what it was Luke had been doing during the penniless period of apprenticeship around the English midlands. 'When we came back to Dublin on holiday, we'd hear that Luke was playing in this place or that, and so on. Then I remember going to the Gate theatre. Our da was there; it was the first time I'd heard Luke singing and I couldn't believe it. I was astounded. Our da was very proud.'

The triumph brought them more fame, but it didn't automatically change much. Asked who was their manager at the time, Luke answered casually. 'No manager. Sure, we couldn't have paid anyone. We were playing for peanuts. Played for porter, really.' It was around this time that I first heard Luke singing 'The Hot Asphalt', a great humorous Irish navvy song from England. I knew immediately that Luke wouldn't be easily ignored and was likely to shake the very foundations of the Dublin scene. He combined a sense of Dublin, a working-class instinct and a powerful singing voice. He was a latter-day Jim Larkin with a banjo.

Peggy Jordan introduced them to the Abbey Tavern,

where they played to packed houses for a brief spell before moving across the road to the Royal Hotel. There they remained as the Saturday night fixture for the next few years. There were also playing on Monday nights now in The Embankment in Tallaght, which Mick McCarthy had taken over in 1962. Mick McCarthy was a bricklayer and active member of the Ancient Guild of Incorporated Brick and Stonelayers Trade Union in Cuffe Street. His brother Seán was a songwriter of some repute and Mick was an accomplished raconteur. He had a good Kerry musical and folklore tradition behind him, and had been involved in organising entertainment and musical events for retired trade union members. Like Luke, he was a good left-winger with a great empathy for the music and the crack. The Embankment was an old watering hole for hillwalkers coming in from Blessington and the Dublin mountains on a Sunday evening and a natural centre for a bona fide ballad session. It was Máirín Johnston who suggested to Mick that he talk to Peggy about getting the group to perform there. Peggy told him, as she had told Minnie Scott-Lennon, that he'd have to build an extension to hold the customers. She remembers that he laughed, but she was right again. The Embankment on a Monday night in the '60s was wall-to-wall humanity. Lifts were thumbed all along the road from the centre of Dublin, and busloads deposited the crowds from the city, who spent the night cheering, sending up requests, joining in choruses.

Not long after that, the Gate brought the group in for a concert at which Luke sang the anti-nuclear song, 'The Sun Is Burning'. No one who was there would ever forget it, Peggy says, or the hush that fell on the theatre while he sang: 'The audience was more than an audience that night. It was a congregation, a solemn assembly.'

Peggy promoted the group on two tours that were wildly successful – 'The Rocky Road to Dublin' and an adaptation of the 'Ballad Tour of Ireland'. One of the incidents that became a legendary Luke story took place on tour, when, as Dara Ó Lochlainn reported, 'It was at one of these that an unfortunate imbiber dropped his Guinness-laden parcel in the middle of 'An Chúileann', a sensitive, haunting and plaintive air. Luke roared: 'One thing I can't stand – a man who can't hauld his drink!' This kind of remark was par for the course at sessions, as was the sheer lusty bravado of the performers, with which Luke was particularly gifted. They had great Dublin repartee and performed best when someone was heckling. Their impromptu responses to audiences and their beards and rough-cut appearance created an atmosphere that was totally different from anything else around at the time.

Some very successful concerts followed – in the Shelbourne Hotel on Sunday evenings, with a break carefully timed for 9.30 so the group could slip over to O'Donoghue's for a pint before closing time. A series of concerts was later held in the Stephen's Green cinema, which held up to 1,100 people. Peggy Seeger and Ewan MacColl made their debut performance in Ireland there, in a programme with Luke and Liam Clancy.

Success was always a sporadic thing; fame and favour not to be taken too seriously. In later years, when asked to relate some highlights from this period, Luke answered: 'The time we were deported from Achill Island after a very unsuccessful busking tour, and then within a few days of it being chosen by Aer Lingus and Bord Fáilte to do a promotional engagement in Frankfurt. 'It was a St Patrick's Day concert for Irish Americans suffering from third-generation homesickness. They really lavished their green-coloured beer hospitality on us when they saw the bog of Achill, which was still clinging to our shoes, muddying up their floor. On the plane over, which I think was the first time the others had been in the air, Ronnie and Barney were canvassing the other passengers to find out who knew the Act of Contrition. They found no succour and so had to content themselves with saying it into each other's ears.'

Demand for their services continued to grow, however, and it was at about this point that the group acquired a professional manager, John Sheridan. John is credited with the permanent catch-cry for tours outside Dublin: 'Remember, lads, no stopping for a drink till we're past Inchicore.' The problem of devising a less unwieldy name than The Ronnie Drew Group began to be more pressing, with Ronnie now insisting that it was necessary. The matter was constantly under discussion but in a fairly casual way. Tommy Makem related a story of his first meeting with Luke, Ronnie and Barney, which took place in the grand setting of the Shelbourne Hotel. 'Luke was still shuttling across to England to sing in the small folk clubs there but they were trying to turn four fellows into a proper group and find a name for them. He told me they were thinking of calling themselves The Heads as in 'Howya, Head?', Makem said in an interview after Luke's death.

In the end it was Luke who came up with the name. The story that became a legend claimed this came about as a spontaneous result of his preoccupation with reading – Luke was said to have been exasperated with the discussion one night because it was distracting him from the volume he was engrossed in, and lifting his head in exasperation, he suggested that they should name themselves after the book, which fortuitously turned out to be Joyce's *Dubliners*. Many years later, Luke with his usual candour said this was a pleasant story but a myth. He had actually thought of the name for much more practical reasons. They were all Dubliners, after all, and the word itself was useful for publicity since it was never out of the headlines, as in 'Dubliner robs bank' or 'Dubliner on bankruptcy charge'. (Even at that, it was a chancy business making it stick. As late as July 1964 a memorable advertisement for an evening's entertainment in Mrs Lawlor's ballroom in Naas pictured Luke, Ronnie, Ciarán and Barney with the title The Ronnie Drew Ballet [sic] Group.)

By the autumn of 1963, when The Dubliners made their first and as it turned out fateful appearance at the Edinburgh Festival, the group had an identity that remained with it despite changes in personnel over the next few years. Nathan Joseph of Transatlantic Records met them in Edinburgh and after a lengthy session in a pub somewhere in the Scottish hinterland until the early hours of the morning, signed the four of them up. The first album, *The Dubliners*, was recorded in a London studio in front of an invited audience and it succeeded in putting the group on the circuit outside Ireland.

Following a series of programmes recorded by the BBC and transmitted from Edinburgh, a company called Envoy Productions took the Gate theatre for *The Hootenanny Ballads and Blues Show*, with Alex Campbell, Dominic Behan and The Dubliners – but still under their more familiar Irish name, The Ronnie Drew Group. One of the singers also on the bill was Deirdre O'Connell, an Irish-American who had recently come to live in Ireland. Within a few months, Luke left the group he had recently named and returned to the folk clubs of England, this time in partnership with Deirdre.

CHAPTER FIVE

'When I left The Dubliners for two years I went over simply to be in MacColl's circle. He had this – you wouldn't call it a school, you wouldn't call it a class – it was a gathering of like-minded people, if you like…it was simply to talk about the songs.'

The 'gathering' was the famous circle known as 'The Critics', which grew out of MacColl and Seeger's Singers' Club, the nerve centre of the whole folk revival movement. It convened at that time in the Union Tavern on King's Cross Road every Saturday evening, with regular well-organised sessions. 'The Critics' was formed to explore folk traditions and help train young singers. When Luke returned to that group in the spring of 1964, Deirdre O'Connell went with him; she says it was a straightforward political decision. The evolution of The Dubliners from the backroom of O'Donoghue's to the front line of popular acclaim had not dulled but sharpened Luke's determination to achieve something more than success. 'Luke was very idealistic; also highly intelligent, and deeply committed to his beliefs,' she said. 'He wanted to get his message across through his talents. He wanted to come back to Ireland, but only when he had a repertoire of workers' songs that he wanted to sing.' In my view, Luke had a lot he wanted to say about his own class, the society he grew up in and the one he wanted for his own people.

Deirdre wholeheartedly shared his thinking. From an early point in her theatrical training she had been exposed to the anti-communist hysteria that prevailed in the United States in the 1950s, which did nothing but stiffen an already defiant backbone and her attitude towards repressive and conservative politics. She was born in that part of the south Bronx where it was not unusual, in the '40s and '50s, to grow up without meeting anyone who wasn't Irish. Irish cultural values were the respected norm, so much so that when Deirdre auditioned at fifteen for the prestigious Academy of Dramatic Arts in Manhattan, she was awarded a scholarship but informed that she would have to be 'de-brogued.'

'I didn't realise I spoke any differently from anyone else,' she said, 'and I refused to go there.' It turned out to be a fateful move. She auditioned instead with Erwin Piscator, the German communist who was director of the Dramatic Workshop at the New York School for Social Research, who trained actors and actresses in the system developed by Konstantin Stanislavski, the great Russian dramatist. There, Deirdre was offered a scholarship without reference to her accent. Her success didn't surprise her family, since had been performing since childhood – not as an actress, but as a dancer and *seannós* singer in the English language, for which talents she had won numerous awards at New York feiseanna. Though neither of her parents had a theatrical background, they encouraged her in what was a firm choice of career even at an early age. Piscator was deported from the United States shortly afterwards, a victim of McCarthyism; Deirdre had discovered her life's work.

She came to Ireland on a visit just two years later, and during her stay in Dublin saw an advertisement for a lecture at the old Pocket Theatre on Ely Place, run by Ursula White-Lennon. The lecture was by Professor Dudley Edwards and with what she now calls the 'typical arrogance of youth – I was shy, but not frightened' – Deirdre afterward introduced herself to Ursula White-Lennon in order to discuss stage drama in New York and Dublin. 'Fair dues to Ursula White-Lennon,' Deirdre said. 'She asked me if I was going to set up a Stanislavski school in Ireland. And I said, yes. But I explained that I'd have to go back for a while first, because I'd won a scholarship to the Actors' Studio."

The Actors' Studio in New York run by Lee Strasberg, where Deirdre then trained, was the most famous centre for Stanislavski training outside the then Soviet Union and had produced such names as Marlon Brando, James Dean and Montgomery Clift. It was six years before she returned to Ely Place and knocked on the door of the Pocket Theatre once more, or as she put it, 'when I came home for good.' She found a flat in Drumcondra and Ursula White-Lennon put a few postage-stamp-sized ads in *The Irish Times*. Within a month the first Stanislavski school in Dublin was in operation. 'I didn't know where they would come from, but they came – Tom Hickey, Tom McDonnell, Aine Ní Mhuirí, that first week; Sabina Coyne a few weeks later; Meryl Gourley, Johnny Murphy.' The rates were amazingly low and the days amazingly long – 'eight or ten, twelve-hour days were nothing.'

The need for funds was a constant pressure, which prompted Deirdre to make another fateful move. She walked around the corner to O'Donoghue's and offered her services as a singer in the pub that was beginning to become known for its musicians, among them Luke Kelly. O'Donoghue's rates, as she remembers it, were ten shillings a day plus all you could eat. Not being much of an eater, Deirdre rarely took more than a bowl of soup which she brought back with her to eat in the theatre. Luke Kelly, on the other hand, still had the appetite which had impelled him to raid his landlady's kitchen several years earlier. He was also getting only five shillings a day. Deirdre customarily sat at the very end of the back room where the musicians held court and Luke well up at the front. 'We were both very aware of each other from the beginning,'she said.

It was Luke who initiated the first conversation, approaching Deirdre to ask why she was getting paid twice as much as he was. Deirdre thought about mentioning the disparity in what they consumed in benefits in kind, but decided against it. Poverty, however, proved to be a crucial factor in their relationship. Since neither could afford the fares over to the northside after O'Donoghue's closed, they walked home together. They also spent a good bit of time in the Pike Theatre in Merrion Square, where The Dubliners rehearsed and Deirdre McCartin, who later married Ronnie Drew, ran the coffee shop. They began performing together occasionally, in the Grafton cinema at the midnight concerts and other venues.

By the time the *Hootenanny Ballad and Blues Show* went on in the Gate Theatre in 1964, with both Deirdre and Luke – as a member of the newly-christened The Dubliners – on the bill, they had decided to stay together. They moved to Finsbury Park in London, where they had a flat off the Seven Sisters' Road, around the corner from two of my brothers, Sean and Tom. Deirdre reorganised her classes in Dublin so that she could teach in concentrated sessions, commuting back and forth on a fortnightly basis.

She also worked in London's Unity Theatre, a workers' enterprise and a favourite haunt of mine. It was subsidised by the Camden Borough Council and located in the heart of the Irish community which stretched from Kilburn to Finsbury Park and Holloway. Camden Town itself was like a thirty-third county of Ireland. Standing on the road in the early morning, you'd see a convoy of enormous steel-gray lorries with Murphy on the front, pulling up to collect the Irish labourers waiting to go off for work on building sites. When the Irish emigrants raised the cry of 'Give us back our Six Counties' in English company in those innocent years, the reply was always 'Give us back Camden Town'.

Luke joined 'The Critics' to serve his time with MacColl, whom he never failed to acknowledge as the greatest single influence on his musical development. When I referred to Luke's 'apprenticeship' in 'The

Critics' group to Peggy Seeger, she was quick to say: 'We were all apprentices there. It functioned as a kind of self-help group to develop each other's potential.' She spoke of Luke's very strong political commitment in those days, of his exceptional versatility and ability to sing many different types of songs and the way he could 'sink into a song', as she put it. 'We all loved him very much,' she said. 'When he sang at his best, he was like a combination of Dickens, Joyce – and all that's best about Ireland.' But like others, Peggy Seeger believes that the very success of The Dubliners was bound to have a damaging effect on Luke. On Luke's return trips to London in later years, she and Ewan saw the effect of the drink problem Luke was later so candid about, and also the effects 'of too much strain on his voice and too much shouting; it took something from his performance.' He was at his best, in her opinion, in those early years, 'soft, warm and personable in his singing...when Luke was singing a good song, you could feel the hair rise on the back of your neck.'

From the time he began to immerse himself in folk music, Luke had singled out MacColl as a kind of mentor. 'I saw him from afar,' he said. 'He was a sort of cult figure. If you didn't know him very well, you tended to be afraid of him because of his reputation. But when I finally got to the man I found him very generous with his time, with his songs.'

MacColl is the man who started the fashion – at least among English folkies, for I'm told it is also the accepted position for barbershop quartet singers in America – for singing with the right hand curved protectively around the right ear, to ward off extraneous noise. It was, I suppose, a variation or maybe an advance on the style referred to by Joxer Daly as 'shut-eye ones', where the singer closed his eyes to look deeply inward and avoid the distracting stares of the audience. MacColl was of Scottish parentage and grew up in the industrial town of Salford. His real name was Jimmie Miller, but like many of the Scots writers and poets who initiated the Lallans movement in the 1940s to promote Scottish literature, he took the name of a Scots poet from the past. His family background was free-thinking, radical, and musically rich in the Scots tradition, and after he left school at fourteen he earned a living as a street singer among the usual assortment of short-term jobs.

MacColl's first interest was drama and with Joan Littlewood, who was his first wife, he was involved in the workers' theatre movement during the '30s and '40s. He always had a great facility for writing musical sketches: 'Dirty Old Town', one of his best-known and loved songs – which later became a Luke Kelly standard – was dashed off to cover a change of set in a 1951 production of 'Landscape and Chimneys' for the MacColl-Littlewood group, Theatre Workshop. Joan Littlewood went on to produce Brendan Behan's *The Hostage* in a controversial production that turned the West End on its ear. MacColl also wrote numerous scripts for the BBC, acted and wrote plays of a standard to draw an accolade from George Bernard Shaw, who said in 1947: 'Apart from myself, MacColl is the only man of genius writing for the theatre in England today.'

Many of MacColl's literary associates, such as the Scots poet Hugh MacDiarmid, were horrified when he turned his full attention to the folk music revival, considering it unworthy of his talents. Apart from his pleasure in the music itself, however, MacColl was spurred by political motives, for he saw folk music as a catalyst for the class solidarity which was essential for social change. He turned to writing songs in the folk idiom and became a household name in Britain with his radio ballad series – among them *Song of the Road, The Travelling People* and *Singing the Fishing,* which won the 1960 Prix Italia. MacColl's best songs, such as 'The Shoals of Herring' and 'Freeborn Man' became classics. Luke never failed to announce MacColl as the author of these and other songs which became very much his own, such as 'The Lag Song' and 'Schooldays Over'. Even 'Paddy on the Railway' which MacColl didn't write, Luke sang in the arrangement MacColl had created.

What is probably MacColl's most famous song – and the only one which earned him any substantial money – is 'The First Time Ever I Saw Your Face'. It became a hit when Roberta Flack recorded it, some fifteen years after it was written. Luke Kelly was in 'The Critics' group the first night it was performed, by Peggy Seeger. It made a profound impression on him. 'He wrote the song for Peggy, Luke said. 'It's the only song which I actually heard once and learned completely, like a palimpsest. It just stuck in my head, verse for verse…it's only three verses so it wasn't too hard, but it's the only song that's ever happened to me with.'

According to Deirdre, Luke was a conscientious student, completely dedicated to what he was doing with the MacColl group and a very powerful performer from the start. 'Luke was challenging, disturbing; he always ruffled a few feathers.' The method of study MacColl and Seeger employed with 'The Critics' was, curiously but appropriately, based at least in part on the Stanislavski system. Stanislavski rejected the standard formula for training actors, which confined itself to teaching techniques to those who either could add the mysterious component of talent or couldn't. He believed that actors and actresses must train to communicate genuine emotional states by undergoing a gruelling but systematic process of self-analysis. One of Stanislavski's approaches was to apply the idea of 'if' to a role, changing the perspective of the actor to interpretation. In 'The Critics', ballad singers were urged to approach a song from the viewpoint of different characters who might figure in it, in order to deepen their understanding of the ballad content.

There is certainly evidence that Luke took practice seriously, with occasional unforeseen consequences. Fintan O'Toole, in a piece on Ewan MacColl in *Magill* magazine, recounted a story MacColl told him of Luke while he was on tour in Scotland: 'Luke Kelly was in the shower when the nice Edinburgh couple with whom he was staying – a doctor and his wife – started to hear strange noises, strangulated throaty sounds coming from upstairs. "My God", they thought, "he's an epileptic and he's having a fit." They rushed upstairs and shouted through the door at him but got no reply except the same throaty sounds. "My God", they thought, "he could be drowning in the shower." They kept calling and getting no answer. Eventually they smashed down the locked door and found young Luke Kelly standing under the shower practising the vocal exercises which Ewan MacColl had set for him: 'Mee, mee,mee, ahh, ahh, ahh...'

Fintan quoted MacColl on Luke: 'He came to us a raw young fellow but he developed with great speed into the kind of singer he became famous as.' MacColl's fear for Luke was, however, 'that the very strength of his voice might make all songs sound similar, subsuming everything into its own sometimes raucous power. '

To earn a living while completing his self-imposed apprenticeship, Luke travelled the folk circuit around Britain, picking up gigs where he could. He and Deirdre frequently performed together at folk clubs, having mighty arguments, as Deirdre recalls, about what to sing and how. They also made a number of discs for Topic Records: 'That was the way you did things then,' Deirdre said. 'You didn't even think about it. There was the mike and you stood up and performed.' Luke also pursued acting, under the auspices of Centre 42, a workers' theatre and arts group founded by the labour movement under the direction of the playwright Arnold Wesker, and named after Resolution 42 on the Trade Union Congress agenda which set out the terms for its establishment. Bruce Dunnett, Centre 42's national organiser for folk music, knew him well in those years and also gave him work at the Scots House in Cambridge Circus, a folk club on a par with the Singers' Club, where Luke got ten shillings for a night's performance. Bruce's recollections of Luke have a good bit to do with drinking and arguing, both of which Luke thoroughly enjoyed, he said. Like everyone else who knew him, Bruce thinks of Luke in terms of books – including three on his shelf to this day, he said, by Smollett, left behind long ago after a night of liquid argument and song.

Politically, Luke was in a world in which he was very much at home. Apart from his friends in the music and theatre circles, he had many others among the Irish political and trade union activists in London, among them my brother Sean. He often drank with like-minded emigrants in Finsbury Park pubs; a particular haunt with good music on offer was a place called The Favourite off the Holloway Road. Luke was especially friendly with Max and Ina Sylvester, who also took Brendan and Dominic Behan in hand on other occasions. Max was a close friend of my own family and stayed with us in Dublin, though on his first visit here I remember that he noted gloomily that there was no 'Monto' and that the nightlife was nothing like what *Ulysses* had led him to expect. He had a well-established small business in Soho and, being one of the rare left-wingers with that kind of collateral, he was on frequent call to bail out ne'er-do-well Irish comrades – sometimes literally, when they broke the law, which seemed to be often enough at the time. I remember a wonderful 'Robbie Burns' night in Max and Ina's house, where the poetry and songs of Burns and other Scotsmen, such as Hugh MacDiarmid, were liberally interspersed with Irish republican songs and anthems of the British labour movement – an interesting combination, which might yet hold the key to a long-term accommodation between our peoples. Years later, when The Dubliners were on tour in London, Luke often slipped away from whatever good hotel they were ensconced in to stay with the Sylvesters.

Deirdre points out that Luke never hesitated to say he

was a card-carrying communist, though she said it certainly affected his career. It caused difficulties going to America, although Luke, like any other genuine left-winger, had no problems with ordinary Americans. He got on very well with Deirdre's father, who held views that were in essence very similar, she said. He made the trip to the States numerous times in later years, but the first trip was with Deirdre to the Newport Jazz Festival, where they performed together. They also shared the tent that served as a dressing room, and some lively moments, with the two young American folk singers who were then the undisputed monarchs of the revival movement there, Bob Dylan and Joan Baez.

Luke and Deirdre returned to Ireland in the summer of 1965, and although Luke continued to visit the British folk clubs for the next few years on a regular basis, it was a permanent move. They were married in the parish church in Whitehall on 21 June of that year. The witnesses were Billy Cullen, an old friend of Luke's from the early days in O'Donoghue's, and Sabina Coyne, one of Deirdre's first Stanislavski students, who later married Michael D Higgins; the reception, naturally enough, was in the Royal Hotel in Howth, where The Dubliners were now performing every Saturday night. Their first home in Dublin was a flat in Kenilworth Road, which was filled with newspapers and books. Luke didn't read for relaxation, but for stimulation, Deirdre said. Luke followed international news particularly avidly, and always wanted to visit Cuba; it was one of the few places he never managed to get to. He rehearsed continually when he was at home, working out songs on the banjo. But to relax he listened to classical music: Beethoven and Mozart, and particularly the Russian romantics they both liked, Tschaikovsky, Rachmaninoff, Stravinsky. Not all their guests appreciated it. Deirdre remembered a Scottish folk singer who came to stay for a month and cut his visit short because the music that dominated the Kenilworth Road flat got him down.

Both of them were involved in the reorganisation of the Stanislavski studio. The old Pocket Theatre had now closed and for the next few years the group that Deirdre had nurtured was nomadic, working sometimes from the Shakespeare Society in Fitzwilliam Street and sometimes from the Pike. A nucleus of about a dozen people set up the Focus Theatre, and it was the writer and journalist Declan Burke-Kennedy who found the premises which they have now occupied since 1967. It was a derelict garage in a laneway off Pembroke Street, and it took the kind of imagination that group was gifted with to see that it had potential. They pooled resources and raised money and Mick McCarthy built the theatre, which has remained much as the same as it was on opening night. Michael D Higgins once described Deirdre as 'the greatest single influence on Irish theatre since the 1960s,' and certainly the list of those who got their training in the Focus in itself tells the tale – among them Gabriel Byrne, Olwen Fouere, Tim McDonnell, Rebecca Schull, Mary Elizabeth Burke-Kennedy, Ena May. The names of the founding members are proudly inscribed on a plaque in the tiny coffee bar, and the first on the list is Luke Kelly. What is less known is that Luke was also one of the first students in the new theatre. 'Luke wanted to learn all that – the discipline, the relaxation, the concentration – because he wanted to be in control of what he wanted to say, 'Deirdre said.

Their lifestyles did not coincide very well, and several years later Luke and Deirdre agreed to live separately, but they remained very close. She speaks of him readily in the present tense: 'He is still part of everything I do,' she told Joe Jackson in an interview in *Hot Press*. 'He is the most special person in the world and that includes my parents, but I'm sure they won't mind my saying that. That basically is all I have to say...Luke was a very private, very introspective – no, internal – person and would always want that to be respected. And I do respect that.'

She also has her own, very firm, view as to what Luke's extraordinary talent as a performer was about: 'He was an actor. That's what set him apart. It wasn't just his intellect or his politics or his voice. Every song he sang, he interpreted.'

CHAPTER SIX

The dead '50s were behind us then, as we slipped
into a rollicking decade. Luke's head seemed a
symbol of the new freedom...if he'd landed in Peru
they would have taken him for an Aztec god. He
had the love of words and the precise elocution of
a true Dubliner and when he sang he would caress
the tempo of the lyric lovingly against the musical
line in a spine-tingling blend. The first three words
he would open with in a song gave him command
of his audience.'

Ulick O'Connor, memoir in *The Sunday Independent*,
February 1984

As Luke remarked, 'The Dubliners when they started out
were revolutionary. They did something that nobody else
had tried.' But revolution was just beginning to be in the
air when The Dubliners came together; Ireland was
succumbing to change that could not be delayed any
longer. John F Kennedy's visit in 1963 had an interesting
impact on the national psyche – and so in quite a
different way did the Beatles' visit that same year,
greeted with a wild exultation that indicated that
Ireland's young people were on a wave-length with their
own generation everywhere, and not a separate and
protected species. Sean Lemass as Taoiseach had set a
new agenda that would have far-reaching consequences,
stirring uneasiness, hope and fear in the country, and his
historic 'hands across the border' meeting with Captain
Terence O'Neill was a clear watershed.

It seemed the most natural thing in the world that five
very different musicians with quite different talents
should join forces and, without effort or planning, create
something unprecedented, because musically a new self-

assurance was apparent. Frank Harte traces this maturing to Ó Riada, who, he says, gave us 'the acceptable face of being Irish, the one you could put on in the drawing room. Ó Riada made Irish music something you could listen to in a dress suit. They listened to it in the Cork Opera House...music they'd have fucked you out of the pub for, until someone came along and told them it was all right to listen to.'

The Dubliners were also very much in line with the Irish tradition of the virtuoso performance. They were in some ways a collection of loners, of whom Luke was the most obvious. The *Irish Press* journalist Con Houlihan, writing in the notes to the first memorial concert for Luke after his death, said 'It may seem paradoxical that such a 'bird alone' should gain fame with a group – but The Dubliners were less a group than a *meitheal.* In the old peasant pattern the *meitheal* came together to do a job – and that was it. The Dubliners were all individualists – Luke and Ronnie and Ciarán and John and Barney were leaves from different trees, blown together by the wind that changed the world of music a generation ago. What they had most in common was artistic honesty.'

In The Dubliners' case, the lack of fine polish or musical arrangement was an advantage; their acoustic sound, obvious enjoyment and ready response to an audience was their strength. They had the total spontaneity that was natural to the streets of their city. Luke explained it simply: 'As we met individually we were already more or less established in our own repertoire and styles. No way can you marry my voice and Ronnie's in a harmonic duo; there's just no way you can do it. We certainly never sat down and wrote out arrangements. It was a growing thing.' Phil Coulter has assessed it in another way: 'I have often tried to analyse the appeal of The Dubliners. It wasn't merely that they were all individually talented; it wasn't just that each was a character in his own right; it wasn't even that they were the first. It was all of those things and more. When those five guys walked on stage something magical happened. They weren't a ballad group; they were a national institution. Twenty years before the music business discovered the phenomenon of 'street credibility', The Dubliners had mastered it.'

The group that Luke had christened and then left in 1964 adapted easily enough, adding Bob Lynch to its ranks and continuing to play at the Royal Hotel in Howth while extending its contacts in England, but it was not yet professional. Those who had 'the day job' still kept it, though it became increasingly difficult. Barney McKenna and I were both working in the engineering section of what was then the Department of Posts and Telegraphs. I was on the fitting staff and Barney with the overhead gangs – not the most suitable employment for a musician suffering from constant fatigue and hangovers after late-night sessions. After a few too many slips on the telegraph pole, he was irrevocably drawn to the world of full-time entertainment.

Barney is one of nature's gentlemen and a magical banjo player, and indeed I believe he launched the whole banjo-playing movement in the traditional area which had faded since the 1930s, when the Flanagan Brothers recorded traditional music in America with a mixture of the gypsy minstrel style and Leitrim-Sligo fiddle-playing. He was certainly the first banjo player I heard who could play traditional music with a consistent deep tone and perfect rhythm, combining the grace notes and inflections of older players with a modern interpretation. He's also a pleasure to watch, with his fingers dancing skilfully and nimbly on his instrument. Luke once said in an interview that he was not a musician in the real sense, as Barney was: 'He's got music running in his veins. Give him any instrument and he can play it.' And indeed, even now a conversation with Barney is like a multimedia experience, as he picks up a melodeon or banjo or whatever instrument is near to hand and plays while he talks, interspersing comments with snatches of music. He comes from a very musical Trim family and was taught the mandolin by his Uncle Jim – who is still playing strong himself at eighty years of age – when he was only five. The legend has it that he learned the hard way, and broke the strings on his Uncle Jim's mandolin and his Uncle Barney's fiddle as well as blowing his father's melodeon out of tune as he mastered his instruments. At twelve he tried to join the Number One Army Band but was turned down for faulty vision. By then, he had taken on the banjo.

Like Luke, Barney left formal education behind after primary school and worked as a kitchen porter, builder's labourer, and furnace worker, playing music all the time. Traditional musicians were still a backroom breed when he was a teenager, frequently unable to find a venue for their sessions, and given that discouraging atmosphere, it's amazing how many persisted. The traditional music scene in Dublin had many fine players, some from Dublin and some from other parts of the country, and I remember such musicians as the Potts family, Sean and James Keane, Mick O'Connor, Mick Hand, Ciarán, Eoin and Maire O'Reilly, the Rowsomes, Leon and Liam; Sean Seery, Vincent Broderick, Mick Tubridy, Johnny Keenan, the Furey family, Timmy Lyons, John Kelly, Tony MacMahon and Sonny Brogan, the famous accordionist who was a great mate of Barney's and himself a storehouse of music. There were also some inspiring musicians, such as John Egan from Sligo, who played with a beautiful, easy style that forced you to listen to the melody and not just the beat.

Somehow or other, we managed to find places to meet, sometimes with great difficulty – I was part of a group that eventually resorted to the waiting room in Connolly Station in Amiens Street. In Donnycarney, Paddy Moloney's home was the centre on Wednesday nights for a group that included Barney and his uncle, Martin Fay and others from the northside. There were others, such as Séamus Ennis, Dan Dowd and Matt Kiernan also attending regular sessions.

Barney went off for his stint in England like the rest of us during the '50s and on his return caused quite a stir in the Pipers' Club in Thomas Street by turning up in search of a traditional session wearing a red shirt, black lace tie and winklepickers. Admittedly he didn't yet have a beard, but even so he didn't look remotely like a traditional musician was supposed to look, and he was challenged at the door by a committee member. He had to prove himself by lilting a reel. His marvellous banjo-playing very rapidly secured his place not only there but anywhere musicians gathered. Barney was always one of the most popular characters at a session , with his unique philosophical outlook. Over the years of fame, he's been singled out in a hundred stories as the eccentric purveyor of what the group calls 'barneyisms' – such as the time he had to kick a hotel door down because he'd locked himself out, but considerately removed his shoes so as not to waken too many guests, or the time he replied to a complaint from Finbarr Furey about his driving 'You think this is bad; you'd want to be with me when I'm on my own.' His distrust of aeroplanes was legendary, as was his disregard for formality or convention; he still has a soft spot for the American Indians and their way of life, and actually meeting his first Indian was the highlight of Barney's first US tour.

As Barney remembers it, he joined the circle in O'Donoghue's at an early stage, when Paddy O'Donoghue was still prohibiting music on the premises during drinking hours because he was worried that this wasn't legally permitted without a licence of some sort. Among those who used to play through the 'holy hour' as it was then, from 2.30 pm to 3.30 pm, were Johnny Moynihan and of course, Ronnie Drew.

Many attempts have been made to accurately describe Ronnie Drew's rusty, croaking and mysteriously melodic voice, but it is probably true to say that it does defy description. Ronnie himself when asked about it in an interview said, 'I'm not sure whether it's a blessing or a curse, but at the moment I'm making a living out of it.' The secret may be that he was a boy soprano who had to give up hymns and choirs when his voice broke. Ronnie, too, had a chequered working career. He began serving his apprenticeship as an electrician but left that for a rapid succession of jobs as a draper's assistant, dishwasher, telephonist. His quick and impudent wit has always been one of The Dubliners' on-stage resources, and no doubt it helped him survive the tedium of those jobs; as a telephonist, he once charged a woman caller tuppence for an overseas call, assuring her there was a sale on. On another occasion, as he related on *The Late Late Show* celebration of The Dubliners' 25th anniversary, he was rather short with a pompous woman who was trying to get priority on a call to England. She grandly asked if he knew who she was, and announced she was the wife of a government minister. Ronnie in reply asked whether she knew who he was; when she said she didn't, he said, 'Thanks be to Jaysus for that,' and pulled the plug on her.

Ronnie did not seem destined for the ordinary working life any more than the rest of his colleagues in The Dubliners, and it was only a matter of time until he took himself and the guitar which was his hobby to Spain for three years. He returned to Dublin, John Molloy, the Gate theatre and the burgeoning ballad movement. The thought of Spaniards spouting Ronnie's inimitable English is one to relish.

Though never renowned as a singer or considered as skilled a musician as the others, Ciarán Bourke's contribution to The Dubliners was an important balance, and his 'Peigín Lettermore' and exuberant whistle playing were always distinctly enjoyable. Ciarán came from a background which encouraged an interest in the Irish language. His father was a doctor, and as a child Ciarán had an Irish-speaking nanny; he was educated through

Irish in Colaiste Mhuire in Parnell Square before he went to UCD to study agricultural science. My earliest memory of Ciarán is of his very hairy beard appearing out of the hay in a farmers' barn where a number of us had found refuge for the night during an early fleadh. Ciaran was one of the first Irish 'beatniks' who developed a love for traditional music and all the crack it represented, a big burly fellow who was gentle and enthusiastic about good company and good music. I always associate Ciarán with the natural Irish tendency to seize today and celebrate it without a care for tomorrow –

Ólaim puins is olam tae
'S an lá na dhiaidh sin ólaim toddy
Ni bhím ar meisc, ach uair sa ré
Mo ghrása 'n déirc is an té do cheap í.

The new foursome had some adventurous times. They performed on a number of televised ballad programmes and then embarked on two dramatic projects, *The Burglar's Opera* and later *O'Donoghue's Opera* under the direction of the television producer, Kevin Sheldon. The theme of the former was that old Dublin street song, 'The Night Before Larry Was Stretched', and for years afterward a portrait of Ronnie Drew, who played the unfortunate Larry, hung in the main bar in O'Donoghue's, his head neatly circled by a noose. Another Hootenanny show followed in the Gate. The first album had brought the group into Cecil Sharpe House, the London headquarters of folk music, and they rapidly became part of the new wave in Britain, starring at the Cambridge Folk Festival and booked for folk clubs across Britain. As Luke said, 'The English folkies always loved us.' They recorded *Folk Festival, Festival Folk* – an offshoot of the Edinburgh Festival – with several other groups, including the Corries. They then recorded *Irish Night Out*, a live performance with such others as Margaret Barry, Michael Gorman, far better known in the London pubs than here, and Jimmy Power. The Dubliners concluded their performance with an Aberdeenshire song, prefacing it with the comment that it probably originated in Ireland anyway. Luke, who was at this point sometimes with the group and sometimes not, played on the same billing, doing several tracks with Dave Phillips, his old friend and colleague from Birmingham.

Luke was also with his old team for a once-in-a-lifetime concert in the National Stadium with Pete Seeger as the special guest. Luke contributed some of his most famous songs that night – 'The Foggy Dew', 'Come To the Bower' and 'Monto'. (This last masterpiece of Dublin satirical comment is the work of the late George D Hodnett, himself one of Dublin's great characters. As well as being a superb jazz musician and musical scholar, 'Hoddy' will be remembered as one of the defenders of Georgian Dublin who squatted in Hume Street in defiance of the property speculator's bulldozer. For this feat he was rewarded with a silver Georgian spoon which he wore proudly in his lapel from then on.)

It was about this time that a fifth musician was added to the team, although as John Sheahan tells the story, he was never officially asked to join. John is the only member of The Dubliners who has had musical training, a point he was said to be rather proud of until the day an old man down the country asked him, 'Tell me, do you read music or are you gifted?' He is from Marino, which he later commemorated with the 'Marino Waltz', and had some musical background in the family; his father was a garda from Limerick, and one of John's prized possessions is a chanter fashioned from a police baton – a very worthy use for such a dangerous instrument, in my opinion. John's father introduced him to Matt Kiernan, Dan Dowd and John Kelly, the great Clare fiddler who played with Ó Riada and the Chieftains. He was greatly encouraged by a Christian Brother called Jim McCaffrey in Marino, where he played in the school band with Paddy Moloney, Leon and Liam Rowsome. He then went on to study for five years at the Municipal School of Music in Dublin, winning awards at numerous feiseanna, although his teachers didn't always approve of his propensity for improvising on the music; he would be reproved with the remark: 'You're composing again.' John was very much influenced by the fiddle-playing of Sean Maguire of Belfast, a master of the art with a creative northern style. I first heard him play in Church Street, where Matt Kiernan had encouraged him to go, and where he picked up new tunes and developed a feel for the more traditional style of Sligo-Leitrim. He brought a beautiful tone and quality to his playing, and I found his classical and orderly style quite a contrast to that of Tommy Potts, another 'master' who also played the occasional set of tunes in Church Street in his own innovative style.

Before he fell in with The Dubliners, John had played with various bands and as a session musician on recordings made by other musicians. On *The Late Late Show*, John explained that he was working in a good, permanent-and-pensionable job with the Electricity Supply Board, having progressed from electrician to draughtsman, and playing as a leisure pursuit. Bob Lynch persuaded John to play with him. Initially they performed as a duet, and being basically shy, John only gradually adjusted to public performances. 'At the time the lads were doing Saturday night gigs out at the Royal Hotel in Howth,' he said. 'I filled in at the interval a couple of times. We were enjoying the crack and people were saying "The new fiddle player sounds good" so Ronnie would say "Are you all right for next week?" and I'd say "Yeah, grand".'

Things went on like that for some time, but the decision to become full-time professionals was becoming more urgent for the members of the group and John discovered that he had run out of annual leave. 'So we decided we'd have a big meeting to discuss the future. The meeting was actually held over a number of pubs, but it started out in Toner's. After awhile there was some bit of a row between Ronnie and Barney; anyway, I can't remember what it was about. But suddenly I realised that what was actually happening was that the group was breaking up right in front of my eyes. And me after packing up my good job that very day. So Mother of God, I was driving home, the group was finished and that was it; you could all do what you like.' The next day as usual John got a phone call from Ronnie enquiring whether he was all right for the following Friday night in Thurles. John replied that he was under the impression that the group had broken up the night before, whereupon Ronnie answered 'Don't take any notice, that happens every week.'

Bob Lynch dropped out soon after. Luke Kelly returned, and so the core of five that was to be the most famous ballad group of its time was established. From the start, the cutting edge of Luke's distinct character was obvious. For one thing, the addiction to the printed word which he had acquired in his first sojourn in the English midlands made him a talking point in the musical world. Luke was never seen without a book in one pocket, a magazine in another and several newspapers under his arm. He would pay a quiet visit to a pub for, as Ciarán Bourke once remarked, 'nine pints and nineteen papers' – or perhaps it was the other way around. In any case, he began the day by devouring a large dose of newsprint and never let the possibility of a spare moment arise without having available further information to fill it. Over the years various other members of The Dubliners have been credited with the remark that you could give Luke anything at all to read: 'He'd read wallpaper,' or 'He'd read brown paper.'

He was not only immensely knowledgeable about world events; he was intensely interested in discussing them, getting into endless enjoyable arguments; and, most important, in doing something about them. His was a practical as well as an ideological commitment, and

Luke instigated as well as responded to calls to serve causes. One of the early efforts was a highly successful concert in the Gaiety Theatre, in aid of what was then the Itinerant Settlement Committee, and a wide range of musicians and singers was rounded up to perform to a capacity house. The highlight of the evening, Joe Kennedy wrote in his column, was 'the impromptu rave-up of "The Twenty-Third of June" by Tommy Makem, Luke Kelly and the American jazz singer Jon Hendricks – Hendricks, in Ireland for a brief singing holiday, scatting the improvisations during the lol-de-fol-de-day choruses.'

Gerry Fleming met Luke in O'Donoghue's, and remembers the first time he heard him sing 'Raglan Road' one Sunday morning in the pub, 'bringing everyone to a full stop, including Paddy O'Donoghue – and believe me, knowing Paddy as we did, that took a bit of doing.' Gerry was a close friend of Liam and Seamus Mulready, whose family Luke had stayed with in Birmingham; Liam was in Dublin then, and with Gerry, a founder member of the Connolly Youth Movement. 'Apart from being a great singer, Luke was highly articulate and a well-read socialist,' Gerry recalled. 'He had introduced great social content into his repertoire and indicated from early on that he was willing to assist the party. ' On a practical level, when Gerry was made redundant in 1966, Luke was quick to provide him with work on the apartment that he and Deirdre had moved to. 'I remember, during the time that I worked there, how Luke regretted the fact that he had never met Brendan Behan...however, he was friendly with the family, Stephen, Rory, Dominic and Sean.'

His assistance wasn't always as useful to his left-wing comrades as they hoped. Mick O'Riordan has a rueful story of electioneering with Luke: 'We had met on his return from Britain and shared a personal-political friendship. When I stood as a party candidate the help of Luke in his artistic capacity was invoked. We billed our public appearance at the then waste ground at Dublin's

Mr Kelly with his family: (from left) Paddy, Luke (with plaster) Mona, Bessie and Jimmy (in his arms)
Sheriff Street, 1940s

(Family album of Luke's brother John)

Home Farm, Under 14 years, 1955. Back row: M Conroy, B Dixon, E Farrell, B Shakespeare, J Whelan, T O'Connell
Front Row: J James, T Lynagh, D Synnott, Luke Kelly, P Bonham

Luke (on right) enjoying his food and listening to a
tune at a 'Songs and Socialism' gathering in Bewdley,
1962
(Mulready family album, Birmingham)

Luke with friends in Bewdley, 1962, including Liam
and Seamus Mulready
(Mulready family album, Birmingham)

Luke and many other friends at the wedding of Des's brother Hugh, 1968. Beside Luke is the bride, Mary Hughes; behind him is his brother, Jimmy Kelly; and in front of him is Mary Maher. The bridegroom is in the back row (5th from right) and Lily, 'mother of all the Geraghtys' is second from left (seated). Behind her (extreme left) is her husband Tom, father of Hugh and Des.

Christchurch Cathedral. That evening a big audience turned up and Luke performed his overture of working class and national rebel songs. The crowd grew even bigger and then with a rousing finale he stepped back to give the floor to the candidate. I went to the microphone, glancing down to straighten my speech notes, and then looked up to find ninety percent of the crowd had evaporated in the wake of Luke! When next we met I greeted him as "Comrade Pied Piper of Hamelin".'

But Luke's primary purpose was still, as Deirdre O'Connell said, to deliver a message through his talents. Luke had brought back from England not only a much enriched repertoire of songs, but the fruits of his own hard work at perfecting his trade. His presence alone was magnetic on a stage, and he had an awesome gift for silencing an erstwhile bawdy crowd. If The Dubliners gave us 'street credibility' before we knew what it was, Luke presented us with 'charisma' before we had a name for it. His voice was always show-stopping, but over the time with MacColl he had mastered the kind of control that could deal with 'The Rocky Road to Dublin' and 'The Galway Races' – two notoriously difficult works for anyone with less than inexhaustible bellows for lungs.

As an instrumentalist, Luke had developed a deliberate style of his own, but had worked alone so long that Barney recollects he had great difficulties tuning his banjo for group work. Luke played a five-string banjo as an accompaniment to his singing, in the style of American bluegrass and the Dixie minstrels. The five-string isn't common in Ireland where the tenor banjo is more favoured by session musicians, though Tommy Makem, Peggy Seeger, Pecker Dunne and Margaret Barry used a similar kind of accompaniment. Nuala O'Connor writes in *Bringing It All Back Home* that it was actually created by an Irish American musician named Joe Sweeney, who added the fifth short-octave string to the four-string instrument introduced to America by the first black slaves – the fifth string working like a drone similar to that on the pipes, to sound a continuous note. To the end of his life, one of Luke's proudest possessions was a Merlin banjo, a present from the Clancy Brothers.

Bill Whelan of the Sackville String Band, who also plays the five-string, told me that Luke learned some of his musical style from Tom Paley, the American folk musician who worked with Woody Guthrie, Pete Seeger and his sister, Peggy, and Ry Cooder, who is recorded on, *Songs From the American Depression*. It was also the musical weapon of the 'Wobblies', (the International Workers of the World) and will always be associated with the nomadic trade union organisers of the early decades of the century in America, who left the great legacy of radical hobo songs and songs of workers' protest. They were the precursors to the songs of struggle and protest which emerged in the '60s. Joe Hill, who was falsely charged with murder, condemned and executed in Salt Lake City in 1917, is of course the most famous, and his output of songs was prolific – 'Casey Jones' and 'The Union Scab' and 'The Preacher and the Slave'; 'The Rebel Girl' and 'There is Power in the Union'. He is best-known for the song about him, written by Earl Robinson and recorded by Paul Robeson. It was a particular favourite of Luke's, one that always inspired workers and human rights activists and it still remains a favourite in Dublin.

The Wobbly tradition of the agitator-cum-organiser-cum-musician has a lot of interesting Irish connections. Many of the ballads are parodies of old Irish songs and hymns; the airs of 'Where the River Shannon Flows', 'Tipperary', 'Johnny I Hardly Knew Ye', 'The Wearing of the Green' all featured in the Wobblies' repertoire with new words written by Ralph Chaplin, Woody Guthrie, Joe Foley, John Healy and Valentine Hukta, or 'T-Bone Slim'. This borrowing of tunes was not just a lazy way out for the composers, but a deliberate tactic to satirise the *status quo*. I am especially partial to 'They Go Wild, Simply Wild Over Me', the Wobbly comment on the legal establishment's attitude towards union activism:

I'm as mild-mannered man as can be
And I've never done them harm that I can see
Still on me they put a ban and they threw me in the
   can
They go wild, simply wild, over me.

They accuse me of ras-cal-i-ty
But I can't see why they always pick on me
I'm as gentle as a lamb, but they take me for a ram
They go wild, simply wild, over me…

Luke's songs gave depth and breadth to The Dubliners' music. They were not a 'political' group and indeed hold differing political views, but Luke's range of songs, with significant content and sung with passionate conviction, ensured that their repertoire would always have something with a social sting in it. Ronnie Drew said of himself and Luke: 'We had no problems over ideology – though coming from very different perspectives, we had a similar view of life and became very close.' The English folk clubs where he had been schooled put a strong emphasis on internationalism. 'If you study the records we've made,' he said, 'the songs I've put down over the years, there's a lot of Scots songs, Burns; a lot of English songs, a few American songs.' Luke and Ronnie often swopped songs, too, depending on whose voice was judged best to do the tune justice, and Luke had also been painstaking in his efforts to amass a large body of Irish music. 'I'm in the unfortunate position of not knowing Gaelic songs, so I can't sing the great Gaelic song, but there are many excellent translations; "Anach Cuan" in translation is a very good song in its own right,' he said.

Another song Luke did very well in translation was 'The Jail of Clonmel' or 'Priosún Chluain Meala', which he got from Liam Clancy, with whom he had a closer friendship than many people realised. In an interview in

Kilkenny years later, Luke remembered learning the song from a book which had the Irish version on one page and the translation on the facing page. He went on to say: 'I first heard it from Liam Clancy. Liam and myself were great buddies altogether, still are. We like the same type of songs because – you wouldn't believe it to hear it now – the voices are quite similar. We like the same kind of songs, love songs, quiet songs. I know I'm known for the big boisterous "Rocky Road to Dublin" and that stuff but my preferences were and still are for the quiet song…when the boys were still together, the Clancys and Tommy Makem, we used to travel regularly around the various fleadh cheoils together and stop off at various boozers and just swap songs. He liked some of the things that I did, and that was one of the ones I more or less learned from Liam; he is a very fine singer indeed.'

The Dubliners in their anarchic way brought together the Dublin character of Brendan Behan, the genuine Irish musical tradition, the entertainment value of O'Casey, the inspiration of Jim Larkin, advocate of the 'divine gospel of discontent'. Tommy Makem said in a recollection of Luke: 'I'd just like to remember Luke throwing back his head and letting a song roar out, any of his songs. He just let them fly. These were songs that maybe had fallen into disuse before The Dubliners found them, but after The Dubliners recorded them they became so commonplace that people disregarded them – songs like 'The Black Velvet Band'.

And it may also be true to say that The Dubliners, by taking what we had and giving it back to us with a fresh approach, gave the nation that boost in self-confidence that laid the ground for the music of the generations that followed them. During the celebrations of The Dubliners' 25th anniversary in O'Donoghue's pub in 1987, with Patrick Monaghan's nostalgic photographs on display, Ronnie Drew made the point that it was not the American tourists who loved The Dubliners. 'It was not their idea of Irish music,' he said of the Americans. 'They had already heard the Clancy Brothers, and we were nothing like them.' Those who came in droves to their concerts were the Irish themselves, and the Irish in Britain, and the Continentals who, as Luke observed, heard echoes of their own traditions in The Dubliners' music.

The group was now on the road constantly and topping the programme at the 'pops proms' at the Royal Albert Hall in London, where the Irish emigrants turned out in their thousands to cheer the boys from home. Their first LP as a reunited entity was *Finnegan Wakes*, recorded live in a revue of the same name at the Gate which was enormously successful. Produced by the actor and director Jim Fitzgerald, *Finnegan Wakes* ran for ten weeks at the Gate, with Luke and The Dubliners, and Seosamh Ó hÉanaí as well. The *Finnegan Wakes* LP remains one of The Dubliners' best, full of the robust atmosphere and audience participation that characterised their gigs. Luke, once addressed as 'you with the woolly head' by someone who was mildly annoying him, retorted 'At least mine is only woolly on the outside.' They were also inventive with off-the-cuff jokes about the state of the country. This is the album on which Ronnie suggests that the way to revive the first official language is to publish the works of all the banned Irish authors in it.

The show itself was a rollicking affair with some wonderful moments: the night after Nelson's Pillar was blown up in O'Connell Street, on 8th March, 1966, The Dubliners produced Nelson's head on stage in the Gate, to tumultuous cheers from the capacity audience. Not long after, The Dubliners issued 'Nelson's Farewell', a witty epitaph, with Luke singing the anthem of the 1916 Uprising, 'The Foggy Dew' on the backing side. The whiff of revolution at the time was heady and still harmless, damaging nothing but an anachronistic concrete monument to imperialism.

DUBLINERS' CONCERT 1966

Declan Collinge

Our eyes are dazed from Celebration*
Our minds too full to think,
Serried tankards line the table
Guinness, Double Diamond,
(The beer the men drink)

We welcome our idol
With rowdy delight
Luke Kelly cheered onto
the stage,
Craggy in fiendish goatee
Haloed by the spotlight
In blasphemous parody,
Loudly singing 'the Monto'
Making our night.

Rainbow fans and gaping doors
Loom before our bloodshot eyes
Night town and its whores
Brazen, Mabbot streetwise,
Loiterers and gaffers
From the Gloucester
Diamond, raucous humour.

Too young to know the lure
Of gaudy dollwoman, we are prey
To comely maidens of the day
Enchantress in hipster skirts
And Mary Quant eyes,
Bluer than blue,
Swinging to the chorus of the times,
'Take her up to Monto
Langeroo! To you!'

From *Fearful Symmetry* (Mentor Publications, 1990)
*This was a popular ale in 1966.

98

CHAPTER SEVEN

I am a socialist. I look forward to a day when I
could sing as an ordinary day's work, as an
ordinary worker. That I'm making money now
doesn't change what I want or what I believe in.
                              Luke, in an interview with Mary Maher
                                   in *The Irish Times*, December, 1967

The Dubliners hit the pinnacle of success from 1967
onward, with everything in the offing from international
tours, double-page spreads in *The Observer*, mentions in
Time magazine, and appearances on the *Simon Dee* talk
show and *Frost on Sunday* in Britain and the *Ed Sullivan
Show*, America's most popular television programme. At
exactly the same period, the movement for social and
political change which had been gathering momentum
through the '60s in Ireland came to the boil in an
outburst of activity that eventually did effect great
changes, though not quite what anyone had in mind at
the time.

The two developments were not unrelated. The song
which made The Dubliners famous was 'Seven Drunken
Nights', an English version of a light-hearted Irish song
that the group had picked up from Seosamh Ó hÉanaí
long before in O'Donoghue's pub. It was released as a
single on St Patrick's Day 1967 and promptly banned on
RTE as offensive to public decency.

Sometime later Seosamh himself gave a straight-faced
interview to an evening paper stating that the song was
about an Irishman who'd worked away from home for
twenty years – a commonplace situation for men from
rural Ireland in those years – and returned to find he had
a full-grown son. And who are we to differ? In fact, the

tongue-in-cheek way in which the song is composed, as the drunken man is persuaded by his wife to accept that the bearded head in the bed is 'her own wee babe' is typical of a sly ambiguity in many Irish songs about sex. Intrigue was added to the incident by the fact that the song actually mentions only five nights, and some play was made afterward of speculation that the 'missing' verses might have been too shocking for even The Dubliners. What was true was that the song had been recorded by Seosamh himself in Irish years before and played on RTE without a murmur of protest; while the Irish establishment were conservative and puritanical in English, they were quite often indifferent to how irreverent and unorthodox our culture was in Irish.

But RTE was already under siege from the technological developments which eventually created the independent broadcasting stations. The national broadcasting network had unchallenged legal command of the airwaves, but couldn't prevent the pirate radio stations, with their emphasis on music, from beaming in to Irish young people. Radio Caroline gave 'Seven Drunken Nights' saturation airtime. The hypocrisy and the foolishness of RTE's decision was too much for a generation already chafing under censorship and prudery, and within two days the record had sold 40,000 copies. It didn't take long to reach the music industry's Silver Disc status, the award for sales in excess of £250,000. The letters pages of the papers were inundated with letters of indignant protest at censorship; the British papers picked up on Ireland's banned song, and not long afterwards, 'Seven Drunken Nights' reached Number Five in the British pop charts.

The Dubliners were heroes overnight, a symbol of the times which were a-changing. The challenge to censorship had been gathering for some time in various fields, most notably among Irish artists. In 1960, quite suddenly, a group called 'Independent Artists' had formed seemingly out of nowhere but in fact out of the frustration of many young artists with the canons of taste imposed by art juries ruling on entries to group exhibits. Their first exhibition stated that the group was 'composed of artists having a lively response to the age we live in', and went on to say 'Independence is not indifference. True independence bears a lively witness to the freedom of intelligence in the face of change...'

The exhibition included works by James McKenna, Edward Delaney, Gerard Dillon. In the mid-'60s such distinguished artists as Arthur Armstrong and George Campbell returned to live in Ireland, and a new generation of art students was gathering in the National College of Art who would rebel against the constraints which dictated 'acceptability'. By that time similar rebellions were taking shape in the universities – 'the gentle revolution', it was dubbed in UCD – and old standards of behaviour were being tossed aside as new demands on student rights were being embraced. The politicians suddenly became aware that something alarming was going on under their noses.

Some took it very hard. One such was Oliver J Flanagan, who blamed television for the advent of sex in Ireland – an odd view of a country which consistently held the record for high birth rates in Europe, when you think of it. But he was at least correct in realising that the influence of the electronic media in shaping that generation cannot be over-estimated.

Whatever about the decision to prohibit 'Seven Drunken Nights', RTE, then coming of age as an independent television station with new young producers and directors, was a real force for change. Ireland now had programmes about social issues and current events – *Seven Days, Home Truths* – and a new young breed of media workers who were not afraid of controversy. The seeds of the explosive issues, leading to the resignation of Bob Quinn, then Jack Dowling and Lelia Doolan as reported in *Sit Down and Be Counted*, were sown in those years.

On the 50th anniversary of 1916, RTE concentrated on a new dimension to history in a fantastic series of programmes that for the first time gave far greater attention to the role of James Connolly than that of Pearse. (The new recognition of Connolly had its connections to the ballad movement, too. While Pearse and Tomas MacDonagh were the acknowledged poets of the 1916 leadership, the labour leader had written a number of agitational ballads based on old airs, the best-known of which are 'The Rebel Song' and 'The Watchword of Labour', which can both still be heard at gatherings of Irish trade unionists.) The historical 'revisionists' began to focus on the social message of Connolly, the leader who placed stress on the role of the working class, the poor and exploited. Throughout his life, Luke belonged to the strain of Irish revolutionary tradition which Larkin and Connolly represent, and he had a scathing contempt for that kind of mendacious new Irish middle class Yeats described so well in the poem 'September 1913':

What need you, being come of sense,
But fumble in a greasy till
And add the halfpence to the pence
And prayer to shivering prayer, until
You have dried the marrow from the bone;

Television also brought to Ireland graphic and immediate news of international events, of a rising militancy among young people everywhere. England had been swept with the movement to ban the bomb – a cause that Luke Kelly always espoused with passion. Ronnie Drew, talking to Elgy Gillespie of *The Irish Times* after Luke's death, made the point that Luke always believed in the songs he sang, brought his ideals from the Campaign for Nuclear Disarmament (CND) into the Dublin bars and 'brooked no falsity'. As well as 'The Sun is Burning' he had a song on the theme with a savagely satirical bent, 'The Button Pusher', often sung at parties in those years by Luke's brother Jimmy as well: ' I am the man, the well-fed man, in charge of the terrible knob...'

In the United States young people took over college campuses and the streets to demand an end to the Vietnam war, a movement with which Luke identified very strongly. He was also a prominent supporter of the campaign opposing apartheid in South Africa, which spread through the '60s from one country to the next across the western world. To the consternation of the more commercially-minded people in the entertainment world, he was never known even to pause to consider the financial consequences of committing his presence and his talents to those causes he believed in. As chairman of Scéim na gCeárdchumann, a trade union group whose aims were to promote the Irish language and Irish culture, I called on him annually to beg The Dubliners' services at the May Day Connolly Concert in Liberty Hall, and the group obliged whenever possible as did many others, among them the McKennas, the Prentice Folk, the O'Donnells from Cork, the Pikemen from Belfast, Ceoltóirí an Chaisleain; Festy Conlon, Bill Meek, Seosamh Ó hÉanaí.

In Ireland the international concerns were taken up along with the pressing social concerns on our own island – for travellers' housing and public housing, the rights of the people to the rivers and lands of Ireland. With our chronic problems of a young workforce and high unemployment – and it was considered bad in the '60s, when the rate averaged about 7 per cent – there was a groundswell of support for the rights of workers which put new life in the trade union movement and created significant turbulence in many hitherto moribund workers' organisations.

The newspapers in those days regularly reported sit-ins and occupations by students and workers, marches of protests and reactions against protests – flags burned outside embassies demonstrating opposition to the

Vietnam war, pickets on Government Buildings in protest against anti-worker legislation, and baton charges, fighting and riots as thousands of Dubliners marched through the streets demanding housing for the families who were crowded in slums or squatting illegally in property bought up by speculators. Debates, pickets, public meetings, occupations and sit-ins were the order of the day, whether against American imperialism or the jailing of the Irish telephonists or the Griffith Barracks campaign to civilise the lives of Dublin's homeless. (Unfortunate husbands and wives were separated in the Dickensian conditions of the barracks because they had no homes available to them.) The largest mass movement of those years was certainly the Dublin Housing Action Committee. This developed as a broad alliance of the homeless, workers struggling for rights, and the left, including in its ranks members of the Labour Party, what was then Sinn Féin, the Communist Party of Ireland (formerly the Irish Workers' Party) student activists and representatives from smaller political organisations.

Such groups proliferated during the '60s. Some, such as the Wolfe Tone Society, were devoted to the discussion of radical ideas; others were groups formed to support cooperative ventures, such as Comhar Linn and Dóchas; some were set up to develop radical cultural awareness, such as the Scéim na gCeárdchumann. Among those which were active were the Connolly Youth Movement, the National Civil Liberties League, headed by Tommy Weldon; Saor Eire, the Socialist Party of Ireland; the Irish Communist Organisation. Students had their own branches or separate political organisations, including the Republican Clubs in UCD and Trinity, the Internationalists in Trinity, later followed by the Maoists. The civil rights movement in Northern Ireland, which so profoundly affected all our lives, was yet to come.

Every group seemed to have its publication, and those interested in new ideas and ongoing arguments could get their fill for a few pence from the *Irish Socialist*, the *Irish Workers' Voice*, the *United Irishman*, *The Plough;* books and pamphlets and material from elsewhere were available from New Books on Pearse Street, run by the Communist Party or the Sinn Féin bookshop on Gardiner Place. The mainstream media were influenced by the launch of *Nusight* under Vincent Browne and the radicalisation of *The Irish Times*, largely under the stewardship of Donal Foley, who had become news editor in 1965. It did seem as if Ireland was finding its soul, moving beyond the suffocating orthodoxy of Catholic nationalism, built on the sanctimonious trinity of the Church, the State and the Irish business class, to a much more socially conscious awareness of class divisions, insecurity, fear, poverty, unemployment. There was fantastic hope, a conviction among young people that they really were going to remake the world. It looked as if, at last, the left was about to take the lead. It did not seem in any way preposterous or even unduly optimistic for the Labour Party to adopt as its slogan 'The '70s will be Socialist'.

The evidence of so much political activity succeeded in rattling some establishment figures. On one memorable occasion, Dublin's Deputy Lord Mayor, Lauri Corcoran, told the annual conference of the Post Office Workers' Union that there were some 3,000 Communist agents active in the city, infiltrating all walks of Irish life, particularly trade unions. He issued a warning to young people on the dangers of communism, to which Gerry Fleming, a good friend of mine and fellow trade unionist now with SIPTU, replied in the Connolly Youth Movement journal: 'While he is at it, he should warn them about the dangers of capitalism, a system which has deprived young people of a decent education and of employment, and has forced one million of them born and bred here to leave...'

The Special Branch put its estimate of dangerous subversives to the *status quo* somewhat lower, as reported many years later, in the early '80s, by Deaglán de Breadún in the 'Saturday Column' of *The Irish Times*. He wrote that the 'real who's who' of Irish life in the 1960s had come to light, a document dated 1969, listing in alphabetical order 226 names, addresses, dates of birth, car registrations where appropriate and physical descriptions of trade unionists, socialists and republicans – two of them, Tomás Mac Giolla and Proinsias De Rossa, then members of the Dáil. (The author of this document was, Mr de Breadún wrote, 'a determined Angliciser, thus the two names appeared as 'Tom Gill' and 'Frank Ross.')

Others selected for mention included: Michael O'Riordan, Gerry Fleming, Joe Sherlock, Máirín de Burca, Desmond Greaves, Proinsias Mac Aonghusa, Fergus Brogan, Sam Nolan, George Jeffares, Paddy Healy, Rayner Lysaght and myself. Certain memory aids appeared necessary, and the descriptions attached to the names were vivid but not always flattering, such as 'short black hair; big ears; pimply face' or 'slovenly gait' or worse still, 'vacant stare.'

While all this new activity was serious and genuine, it was anything but dour. The pubs were as important as venues for debate and organisation as the rather cold, cramped rooms at the top or bottom of union halls where many of these organisations met. Dublin being conveniently small, it was even possible – if you had the stamina – to touch base at most of the 'left' pubs in a single night, though you were likely to be waylaid by interesting company anywhere along the way. Bob Bradshaw, a veteran socialist republican, storyteller and wit, used to advocate the creation of a job for a 'runner,' whose task would be to circulate the various most popular venues on a weekend night, providing an updated list of clientele in each to those who were thinking of shifting on from wherever they were. McDaid's, Grogan's, The Bailey were all off Grafton Street, and a short jaunt up to Stephen's Green would set you on to what was known as 'the Strip,' not in any way to be confused with the Leeson Street nightclub area which later took that title.

The original Strip was largely confined to Merrion Row, from O'Donoghue's within whistling distance of the Shelbourne Hotel to Gaj's Restaurant, presided over by the hospitable and indefatigable Margaret Gaj. Gaj's was an institution in itself, a small restaurant with a steady local clientele who appreciated the home-cooked food and tasteful wood furnishings, and a home from home for young people engaged on any number of political campaigns who held planning meetings there. Sometimes these were formal and organised. Sometimes it was more a matter of arriving late at night, stashing placards and posters in the hallway (or perhaps buckets and brushes, if the project involved a little wall propaganda) and venturing in sure of a good supper and lively discussion with Mrs Gaj and whoever else happened to turn up.

There were offshoots from the main Strip. Gerry Fleming has a vivid recollection of the various watering holes. The Majestic Hotel on Fitzwilliam Street was a good late-night haunt, often frequented by entertainers, including Luke and Deirdre. It was run by Big John Sullivan whose familiar warning was 'No messing, or down the steps on your head.' Smokey Joe's on Molesworth Lane was another favourite for late-night sessions, also a haunt of Luke's. There was Devine's on Baggot Street, which later became the Baggot Inn, and the premises of the Communist Party on Pembroke Lane where revellers often adjourned after closing time for 'subversive' music and ballad sessions.

O'Neill's on the corner of Merrion Row and Merrion Square was another haunt, presided over by the taciturn and unpredictable proprietor who was well-known for refusing service without explanation or, equally, extending great kindness to drunks on the premises. His staff were required to wear long white aprons and his decor was bare, bleak, lit by unshaded light bulbs and uncompromising in its denial of comfort. His patrons loved the place. They included civil servants from Government Buildings around the corner, journalists, Dáil deputies and senators, and a wide range of young left-wingers, particularly from the Scéim na gCeárdchumann and the Connolly Youth Movement; leaders of state and fomentors of revolution rubbing shoulders.

In the midst of all this merry ferment, it seemed only appropriate that a group such as The Dubliners, who were as unlike the usual celebrities of popular music as possible, should rise to heights of recognition and fame. 'Seven Drunken Nights ' catapulted them out of the folk world and into the mainstream, but it changed them not at all. When 'Seven Drunken Nights' reached the bottom rung of the charts at Number 20, someone rushed up to Ronnie Drew to inform him breathlessly of the fact and he replied mildly: 'Is that good or bad?' They were undoubtedly the most unlikely assembly of stars the BBC's *Top of the Pops* programme had ever seen. They were a phenomenon in that world of adulation and hyperbole, and were quite nonchalant about their new status. They still played in pubs at home and in Britain, as they had always done, as well as in concerts at the Royal Albert Hall. As John Sheahan once remarked of the difference, 'You're still playing to people. There's just more of them.' When Luke was asked whether they would like another hit he replied, 'It doesn't matter a damn. When you think of the pressure of bookings and the sort of things people want you to do, it's not an enjoyable prospect at all. If it happened again, I'd rather it was with a song that made it on its own merits, like "The Leaving of Liverpool" or "Navvy Boots".' It apparently didn't even occur to them to change their material to angle for further success in that competitive field. When another single – 'Black Velvet Band', with Luke in the lead – reached the charts, they were surprised. 'We didn't feel it was ideally suited for the

British markets,' Luke said in an interview.

Several interviewers suggested that this casual attitude was due to the fact that as folk singers they viewed pop music with disdain, but again The Dubliners confounded expectations. Luke in particular liked a lot of popular music. He was an enthusiastic Beatles fan, and pointed out that they were nearer to the tradition of folk song, in writing their own material to comment on matters of contemporary interest, than the folk singers. 'The Beatles used to go the Spinners Club in Liverpool, and they were the first to realise how to write popular, rhythmic songs which are danceable and possessed of a tremendous amount of meaning,' he said. He also professed himself a showband fan: 'I love all the blokes in the showband business. They are great heads...I like Earl Gill, Sean Dunphy, Butch, all the lads in the Capitol. Favourite bands? Dave Glover is very good and so are the Capitol. I don't get a chance to hear many of them now.'

By St Patrick's Day of 1968 The Dubliners had become something of an international curiosity and were special guests on the Ed Sullivan show, broadcast coast to coast in the United States. It was a startling new image of Ireland to present to America. The Clancy Brothers had, after all, been country men, wearing uniform Aran ganseys. Five young fellows in whatever clothes they normally wear, singing in undiluted Dublin accents, were a disconcerting development. In ways that couldn't have been foreseen then, The Dubliners stamped the cultural imprint on the world of the authentic, rapidly urbanising Ireland; they were the precursors of what was to come many years later, in Jim Sheridan's *My Left Foot* and indeed in *The Commitments* based on Roddy Doyle's novel.

They also made a major breakthrough for Irish music. Suddenly they were in huge demand, taking off on tours of New Zealand and Australia, as well as the Continent. Over the next few years they were to appear in most of the major halls, and the major telvision music programmes, in Britain, Germany, Holland, Norway, Denmark, Sweden, Finland, Belgium, Austria, Switzerland and Iceland, playing to capacity audiences everywhere. Apart from their regular tours they made regular brief forays into Canada and the United States, including a 1968 tour of the States as part of a group of international artists chosen by Columbia Artists Management each year to present a prestigious educational musical programme. The albums followed, one after another: *A Drop of the Hard Stuff, More of the Hard Stuff, Drinkin' and Courtin, The Dubliners At It Again, The Dubliners Live at the Royal Albert Hall*. That all these titles helped to harden the image of The Dubliners as hard-drinking Paddies bothered no one, least of all themselves.

The association with drink, as Luke said many years later when he had been off alcohol following brain surgery, was almost unavoidable, since most of their gigs were in pubs, and also perfectly accurate, since most of them were adept at holding drink from a tender age. (The exception is John Sheahan, whose standard tipple is a large cola with ice, and who has been met with frank disbelief by fans when he orders it.) But Luke later said that the ready assumption that drink was to blame for any symptoms of ailment may have been a crucial factor in delaying diagnosis of his own illness.

Fame meant that naturally The Dubliners were pursued by the media, covered on tour for the home readers and interrogated on their every passing thought as well as their fundamental values and philosophical beliefs. Luke, who was full of camaraderie and humour and kind to any passing stranger on the street, had a way of not bearing fools too gladly when they impinged on his privacy. But he displayed considerable patience in dealing with provocative questions, pointing out to one journalist who accused him of complying with tawdry publicity-seeking in granting her an interview that he was merely exchanging a service: her newspaper needed a story, The Dubliners needed publicity. He was regularly singled out for persistent quizzing as to whether or not whether or not commercial success had spoiled the socialist in him. The theme runs like a thread through interviews, and the answers were always consistent.

Journalist Joe McAnthony wrote in one piece: 'The steady rise to entertainment fame and the monetary awards accruing from it appear to have left Kelly's private vision unaffected. He is vehemently opposed to the private enterprise system and in the sense that he would sacrifice everything at his command to see it done away with, he is a revolutionary. But listening to him, one has the impression that he is less driven towards the creation of a Utopia than he is reacting against his experiences of life in our society. "You've only got to look around you," he says, gesturing with his arm, "to see the injustice in the system. I'm a socialist because I believe it will change all of that"…How deep is his commitment? 'I would stop singing and work at any job with my hands at any time if I thought it would help to improve things for people. I want to see the time coming when, say, a child will get the opportunity to use his brains. We didn't get that chance and it still doesn't exist today regardless of what people say.'

Anthony concluded: '…A soft person, there is no doubting the sincerity of his views or his desire for the removal of inequalities in Irish life.'

There was also a mounting suspicion among many that there was something positively offensive politically about all this success. The tobacco company representative whom Breandán Breathnach (writing in the journal of Irish music, *Ceol*) quoted so gloomily as predicting that Irish music would become a part of the tourist industry, had been proven quite right. The long-ignored and little-valued customs of singing and making music had become a serious business proposition, a commercial opportunity. But the public embracing folk music were not simultaneously championing the cause of the common man and woman, the political attitudes the folk music revival was seen to represent; the fear was that success would not only corrupt the music itself, it would do nothing at all to promote the good of the common people.

Luke himself had concerns in this area, and clearly gave the matter a lot of thought, as *The Irish Times* interview with Mary Maher indicates: 'The rise and inevitable fall of the ballad movement was not what Luke Kelly, or the other musicians of his viewpoint, envisaged six years ago,' she wrote, and then quotes Luke: 'Done amateurishly, or done over and over again – and I include myself in that, by the way – the songs become devalued. The ballads have become a part of the popular music spectrum, though it was the original idealistic intention to replace pop music with them.' He added, 'And there is still a great deal of idealism in the movement. It's quite obvious which groups have formed for commercial reasons – they get a nice girl in front, and three slickly-clad lads in the back. It's very easy to be slick on stage. But to retain people's interest when you're not dressing up, not making concessions to the – well, the tinsel aspect of show business – is the test; to retain their interest because they think something might happen, because they might hear something.'

In an interview in the *Irish Socialist* at about the same time, Luke took pains to make it clear that popularity didn't indicate anything deeper. 'Public taste is formed by mass media; it has very little will of its own,' he said. 'Therefore when the present economic drive behind the ballads slackens – as it inevitably will – ballads will have become an integral part of the mainstream of light popular music, resulting, most probably, in its separation from the body of the unadulterated ethnic heritage. For the most part, the songs which have become popular are the city songs of not much more than 150 years duration, leaving the Gaelic tradition (with the exception of a few noble but unsingable translations) untouched – but unfortunately, unsung as well. The interest in ballads is skin-deep – not yet inspiring our deep cultural identification with our tremendous national past.'

Later, Luke was quick to appreciate that his predictions had not come true and that music in Ireland had developed in a much more creative way than he had imagined it would. At that time, he felt it important to stress that political change did not come about because a certain kind of music became popular. Asked whether there was any national or social significance in the upsurge of interest in ballads, he replied that while the renewed interest in folk music couldn't be questioned, it had to be admitted that the interest was 'in the main a purely ephemeral one. It has no roots. It was because it became an economically viable proposition to promote these songs – and by extension for the vast number of people, including that great phenomenon the ubiquitous "showband", to learn and sing them – that there is what we prefer to call a revival.'

It was typical of the kind of wide-ranging interview Luke gave that he went on to talk about both music and politics easily.

He listed his favourite ballads in different categories: 'Róisín Dubh' and 'The Foggy Dew' and 'The Rising of the Moon' as rebel songs, and of political songs, Robert Burns's 'Such a Parcel of Rogues in a Nation' and 'Joe Hill'. 'In this field as well, I like Woody Guthrie's Sacco and Vanzetti songs,' he said, adding, 'Love song favourites are too numerous to mention. Bawdy songs (genuine non-prurient variety only admitted) I like, but can afford to give utterance to them only at parties.' His main influences, those he had been able to study close at hand, he named as Joe Heaney, Ewan MacColl, A L Lloyd, Paddy Tunney, 'to mention a fistful,' and then promptly replied that he was quite willing to declare his attitude on Vietnam: 'There are no two sides to it. The

113

Americans are in the wrong – on various levels – and for their own good should cease fire, pack up and go home.'

Sometimes he was called upon to defend The Dubliners from allegations of falsely courting success by their rumbustious image. When The Dubliners released 'Maids When You're Young Never Wed an Old Man' it met the same fate as 'Seven Drunken Nights', although this time there was no official admission of a ban. Just the same, the song was considered too explicitly sexual even in England for the public service airwaves, and again it was left to the pirate radio stations to put The Dubliners before their audience. There were those who suggested that The Dubliners were now catering to a British audience disposed to enjoy this new variation on stage Irishism. Luke's patient reply was: 'The songs were in our repertoire. They're good, solid songs, not great; they can't all be great. It's just an irony of the communications racket that they get banned and therefore famous.'

The evidence is very clear that Luke had an unwavering view of what his work was about, and that fame and fortune did not blur that. He took every opportunity to sing the songs with which he could deliver his message; during a gruelling two week tour of the United States he managed to link up the Veterans' Memorial Building in San Francisco, where the United Nations charter was signed, with 'The Peat Bog Soldiers' – and then, because the year was 1969 and events in Derry and Belfast had world attention, turned it adroitly into something called 'The Bogside Soldiers.' His impact was distinct and meaningful.

But inevitably, The Dubliners' commercial value and involvement on the international circuit had created their own problems. Some of the music and songs had become devalued by repetition, as Luke said, and the group's very popularity meant more and more repetition was demanded. In Luke's case, though, I know he grew more and more uneasy with time and wanted more challenging outlets for his talent, eager to diversify and find new ways of working. John Sheahan points out that despite his serious love of folk music, Luke was neither conventional nor a purist, and was always willing to experiment with new ideas. Eamonn Campbell, who joined the group at later stage, confirmed the point, saying that Luke was always enthusiastic about experimentation. He had no difficulty including a grand piano or a brass band in a performance or varying his own performance to see what came of it – trying a rock song, Dixieland jazz or a general excursion into camping it up.

For a time, it appeared as if at last his long-standing attraction to the theatre would provide the answer he was looking for. The energy of the '60s had caught fire in dramatic circles as it had in the art world. Visiting British street theatre groups and new companies – 7:84 (named because 7 per cent of the people owned 84 per cent of the wealth) and Paint and Ladder created a wave of interest, which was rapidly followed by a kind of Irish dramatic insurrection which eventually launched a renaissance in Irish theatre. 'Project '66' was launched at a packed meeting in the Gate Theatre. Censorship and stultifying convention were challenged by actors, writers and playwrights with some electrifying speeches, notably one by Jim Fitzgerald, who had earlier produced The Dubliners in the *Finnegan Wakes* revue. It was out of this meeting that the Project Arts Centre was established, and run so dynamically for years afterwards by Jim and Peter Sheridan who used to take turns writing new plays and directing them. The Project joined the Focus as the launching pad of new Irish actors, actresses and playwrights, and suddenly small touring theatrical companies seemed to be everywhere, staffed by young actors and actresses who were interested in improvisation, new writing and linking the dramatic arts to local communities. The legacy is very obvious all over Ireland today.

There had always been a Dublin concept of theatre – always good for a song and dance, and more likely than

not to break into a ribaldry on stage to shock conventional attitudes, as Wilde, Shaw, O'Casey, Behan had demonstrated in different ways. Now it was adapted with ease
in the new mood of irreverence, and the new determination to establish a culture of the people. The mood
inevitably caught on in the established theatres, as
anyone who saw the brilliant Abbey production of
Borstal Boy will never forget, with Niall Toibin delivering
an amazing performance as Brendan himself.

In the 1969 Dublin Theatre Festival, Luke went on
stage as Sergeant Kite in the production of *The Mullingar
Recruits*, an adaptation of Farquhar's *The Recruiting
Officer* transposed to an Irish setting – and since Farquhar
had grown up in Ireland and like Congreve and Sheridan
attended Trinity, it made sense to assume he had Irish
settings and characters not unlike Luke in mind when he
wrote his plays. In the innovative spirit of the time, the
producer, Dominic Roche, incorporated recruiting songs
and dances of the period (around 1700) into the script,
stating: 'It won't be a musical exactly; you could call it
an Irish farce with song and dance.' Many of those who
came did so expressly to hear Luke sing, and the general
view was that he didn't do near enough of that.

Much more notice was taken when Luke was cast as
King Herod in *Jesus Christ Superstar*, produced by Noel
Pearson. Phil Coulter recalled in his memoir: 'the look of
panic on Luke's face the first night I counted him in,
flanked by two chorus girls,' at the Gaiety, and Luke
freely admitted he found it far more frightening to go out
of the wings before the footlights than to face a stadium
of thousands with his banjo. But he loved doing the part,
and the critics loved his depraved and lecherous interpretation of the New Testament despot. By 1972 Luke
had been joined on stage by the rest of the group in one
of the most controversial productions ventured by the
Dublin Theatre Festival in those years, *Richard's Cork Leg*,
based on incomplete works of Brendan Behan and
produced by Alan Simpson. The Dubliners cancelled

their engagements to take part, a decision their manager, Noel Pearson, accepted philosophically: 'Their decision, which they are happy about, means that they will lose about £1,000 a week. *Richard's Cork Leg* was a romp, a pastiche of music-hall sketches, jokes, ribald lyrics and songs found among Behan's papers, and it got a mixed and slightly puzzled reaction from the critics when it opened in the Peacock. But it did well enough at the box office to move to Cork, where it was roundly and promptly condemned by the bishop. This did it no harm commercially, and *Richard's Cork Leg* hopped back for a stint in the Olympia Theatre and then across the water to the Royal Court Theatre in London for a month's run.

The English critics were, by and large, not ambivalent in their views: 'All that is worst in the Irish character – the fecklessnes, the disputatiousness, the cynicism and the blarney – has gone into the making of *Richard's Cork Leg*, an entertainment at the Royal Court that does not pretend to be a play,' John Barber wrote, admitting grudgingly that 'Behan's love of people and sex and his heart-warming disrespect for every institution this side of the grave and beyond cannot help but start the occasional guffaw and twinge of sympathy.' Generally, although the 'entertainment' was dismissed, The Dubliners won the critics and the audiences with their customary skill and verve. They celebrated their tenth anniversary as a group as members of the Abbey cast and went back to business as usual with a tour of Britain.

Luke returned to the cast of *Jesus Christ Superstar* for another successful production, but a new career in theatre did not materialise for him; and though he remained as serious politically as he always was, the situation in Ireland was rapidly changing from one of hope and unity across the left to one of confusion, doubt and division.

CHAPTER EIGHT

Con Houlihan, in the programme notes to the first Luke Kelly Memorial Concert in May 1984, referred to a poem written by the great Italian poet Giusseppe Ungaretti for a friend, an exiled Arab whom he knew while living in Paris, which ends: *'E non sapeva sciogliere il canto del suo abbandono '* – He wasn't able to express the song of his loneliness...'

Con wrote: 'Luke Kelly lived much of his life among his own – and yet he too knew a kind of exile: it was the spiritual exile of one who wished for a better world. Luke was luckier than Ungaretti's friend: he found expression for his loneliness. For him, singing was as essential as it was for the American blues singers who found themselves 'lonely and afraid in a world they never made.' Luke brought home to you that singing had been man's primal mode of expression. When language was rudimentary, the musical notes expanded it: man sang before he spoke...

The end of the '60s and start of the '70s proved to be a more traumatic period than the heady earlier years had led us to expect. In some respects it was a time of loss of innocence, as the harsh reality of a divided society and the deeply conservative nature of our Irish upbringing began to reassert itself. When everything had so recently seemed possible and so many young people thought that Ireland had changed utterly, a new and terrible beauty had been reborn in Northern Ireland; or perhaps we had merely unveiled the ugly face of reality. The ferocious reaction of the Unionist establishment to the perceived threat of the civil rights movement – launched so bravely in the early '60s by NICRA, the Northern Ireland Civil Rights Association – precipitated a social, political and cultural seachange.

Like all socialists, Luke was instinctively on the side of the underdog, and in the context of Irish society he understood and identified with the aspirations to a socialist united Ireland. In those first days of confusion and highly charged emotion following events in Derry and Belfast, he was one of many who gathered around a loose organisation known as the Citizens' Action Committee. There were numerous, rather chaotic, but intensely sincere meetings in the upper room of The Bailey and Brian's Bar, off Grafton Street, as this *ad hoc* group struggled with debate about what should be done to meet the crisis. The Dubliners – with the Munroes and Nigel Denver – were among those who donated their services to a massive peace rally organised by the Citizens' Committee in July of 1969 at the Wellington monument in the Phoenix Park. In August, Luke opened a Dubliners' concert in the National Stadium with a stark, passionate recitation of his poem, 'For What Died the Sons of Róisín?', which Hayden Murphy had earlier published in *Arena*, a poetry broadsheet Hayden had launched with Luke's enthusiastic support. (In his memoir of Luke in *The Scotsman*, Hayden wrote that in fact he 'rescued' the magazine at a concert in the National Stadium: 'He sold it to more than 2,000 punters by his passion, persuasion and the threat not to continue until they bought a copy.'

That autumn The Dubliners chose Kilmainham Jail as the venue for the release of their album *Revolution*, produced by Phil Coulter, which uses a piano and bass in the arrangements to stirring effect. In the spirit of the times, the group added new songs to their repertoire. Their collaboration with Phil Coulter produced 'Hand Me Down Me Bible', which Luke sang with great relish, commenting that it was a tribute to a certain Reverend

Doctor in the North; and at a huge rally two weeks after internment was introduced in August 1971 – 'Free The People', in which Phil Coulter said Luke 'breathed life into my words.' The song was released as a single and rapidly became a hit. Two months later, The Dubliners cancelled a concert in Lancashire rather than submit to a request to drop two songs which were old favourites but considered unacceptable in the new climate: 'The Wearing of the Green' and 'The Merry Ploughboy', with its rollicking line about the rattle of a Thompson gun.

But of all the songs of those years the one which has endured is, of course, 'The Town I Loved So Well.' Coulter wrote it with Luke in mind, not only for his voice, but because, he said, 'Luke would bring to it the integrity that any writer looks for.' Luke's recording to this day has the power to move profoundly a generation hardly born when it was written. The song itself is arguably Coulter's best, but in my opinion far too many singers sadly trivialise it into sentimentality. When Luke sang it, it was a masterpiece because he brought his own heartbreak to the shocked, raw verses relating the destruction of home and childhood.

Like all masterpieces, that song and its singer had universal appeal. Little else did as the '70s unrolled and circumstances became increasingly complex. Daily life in Northern Ireland began to ring with the calamitous echo of Clarence Mangan's apocalyptic translation of Róisín Dubh – 'O! The Erne shall run red with redundance of blood' – something quite different from the questions posed by Luke in 'For What Died the Sons of Róisín?'

Slowly and steadily, the common struggle which had united so many and engendered such a spirit of openness and tolerance was overcome by more primitive loyalties, greater introspection and exclusiveness. The first ripples of social division later became shock waves as we were overcome by the tide of violence. The Strip in Dublin was no exception. Many old and valued friends parted as we went in different directions, drank with those of our own thinking in different pubs, and grew deeply pessimistic, suspicious of many who were once trusted comrades.

The Dubliners, like other entertainers, were increasingly affected. The frequent criss-crossing of the Border by showbands, singers, folk groups from South to North and back again, slowed as frightened people returned to their safer havens on more predictable turf. The days when The Dubliners could bring huge audiences of Catholics, Protestants and dissenters together in Belfast's King's Hall to join in choruses of both Orange and green songs were suddenly gone – just as, decisively, were the times when the Miami Showband brought the young on to the same dance floor, far from the bigotry and tribalism of the older generations.

And finally the music itself, once mortar that kept us together, became part of the masonry that kept us apart. Inevitably, the songs became subject to new 'politically correct' judgment. Particular performers were readily identified by their viewpoints and their choice of songs, which assumed different significance. The quality and enjoyment of a performance came to matter less than the politics behind it. Some groups unceremoniously donned the mantle of recruiting sergeant and built a following on an atavistic appeal. Still other groups stiffly rejected much of their own tradition, finding it necessary to renounce all things Irish. The separate strands that had brought the ballad culture to fruition became additional weapons to be used in the ancient conflict. War cries came into vogue and that more generous message of human rights, international links and class solidarity were the casualties.

Witch doctors praying for a mighty showdown
No way our holy flag is going to fall...But hey,
   don't listen to me
For this was meant to be no sad song
   I sang too much of that before...

'The Island' that controversial song by Paul Brady, from which these lines are taken expresses a lot of my own feelings about that era. I hear it as an assertion of common humanity over sectarian violence, a plea for love over the bitter turmoil of prejudice and violence and a rejection of the wail of death.

I often ran into Luke when he was between tours during those years in one or another hostelry. He had friendships with many people whose views I wouldn't have agreed with. But I think Con Houlihan's comment in his memoir of Luke sums him up correctly: 'Luke was a rare Irishman in that he was utterly devoid of prejudice – at a time when tribal emotions were running wild, he never lost his stance as a member of the world's brotherhood...and if he was in any real tradition, it was that of Joe Hill and Vachel Lindsay and their fellow wandering minstrels who sang about man's dignity in the worst years of American capitalism.'

Usually, we talked about what was going on in the trade union movement – industrial changes, strikes, developments in workers' struggles, problems of organisation or political undercurrents. On many, many occasions I was looking for his help in drumming up support by way of concerts and entertainments for one cause or another and he responded generously and without hesitation if it were possible. At no stage did I ever feel that his stature as a public persona or the pressure of international engagements had lessened his involvement with the 'underdogs' at home, the under-privileged people of his city or the world's oppressed.

If anything, he was too easy a mark for strangers. It was one of the hazards of his life in a small city and perhaps a price that had to be paid for public acclaim. All The Dubliners were public property, known by sight around Dublin and addressed by perfect strangers as lifelong friends. But Luke was so highly visible that he was recognised a half-street away and hailed with 'Howya, Luke!' by everyone. He was also genuinely kind-hearted and sociable. The company wasn't always pleasant, and I have seen him use all the street gurrier instincts Dubliners grow up with and his own uniquely quick tongue to rid himself of unwanted hangers-on. Far more often, he was surrounded by friends and well-wishers who were proud of him and loved nothing more than to share a pint and a bit of crack with him in that most amiable ambiance of the Dublin pub.

Luke's habit of accumulating people had its awkward side. Sometimes he brought them home with him, where they might linger indefinitely. On several occasions they overstayed their welcome considerably and caused him great difficulties. He was more than equalled in this propensity for gathering a crowd by Barney, and once, as Phil Coulter vividly recalls, the pair of them turned up at a recording studio for rehearsals with no fewer than twenty-seven 'guests' in tow.

At a glance, a partnership between Derryman Phil Coulter and Dubliner Luke Kelly would seem unlikely. In some ways the two appear to be complete opposites in their personal and musical preferences, yet they developed a strong and productive musical partnership and became very close personal friends. Professionally, Phil found Luke often abrasive and uncompromising: 'We didn't always agree – Luke's version of what we should be doing in the studio and mine didn't often coincide. But his integrity was never in doubt.'

Phil Coulter is most frequently associated with popular music and light entertainment and such major names as Butch Moore, Des Kelly, the Capitol Showband. But his own background is in folk music. He had a group himself at one point called The Journeymen, and remembers Ian Campbell's 'The Sun is Burning' very well. He first heard Luke sing in one of the early Gate revues and at a late night session in the Grafton cinema. When Noel Pearson asked him to become involved with

The Dubliners, he was delighted to take up the challenge. He remembers that when he first met Luke he was wearing purple socks and 'looked like an unmade bed'. In the fashion of The Dubliners, work meant 'in at the deep end, no detailed rehearsal and get on with it.' There was some initial sorting out to do on such matters, but from the start Phil found Luke most forthcoming about ideas for songs and most receptive to new suggestions for arrangements.

Interestingly enough, 'Joe Hill' was one of the first songs they attempted together. Phil introduced a piano, an instrument much disdained by many traditional and folk musicians. After the piano came the bass and later a second guitar for bass in sound recordings. Luke, according to Phil, never saw himself as a 'strict folkie', or carried a torch for a particular musical form. 'He was an entertainer who loved being on stage and capturing an audience with his singing.' When Phil was directing him in *Jesus Christ Superstar*, he said, Luke had to work hard to adapt to the discipline and precision of combining a song-and-dance routine and an orchestra. On the first preview of the show, Luke veered stage left rather than stage right at a critical moment, and threw the entire arrangement into total confusion. But his recovery skills were extraordinary, and he managed to turn the gaffe into an opportunity to steal the show.

During their working relationship, Phil created many new compositions, including such lesser-known gems as 'Donegal Danny' and 'Ronnie's Mare', a genial gibe at Ronnie Drew's equestrian inclinations. Like most working-class Dubliners, Luke thought of horses as symbolic of the social divide Brendan Behan described as 'Catholics, and Protestants on horseback.' Apart from 'The Town I Loved So Well', Phil also wrote 'Scorn Not His Simplicity' with Luke in mind. The song was deeply important to Phil, as it was about his own handicapped child, and Luke himself was so moved by the song that he sang it only once in a public forum, as a guest on a Jim

McCann show. He made a powerful recording of it and sometimes sang it at private gatherings, with Phil at the piano, but steadfastly refused to sing it in concert.

By the mid-'70s The Dubliners were performing less often in Ireland and more and more frequently abroad, especially in continental Europe, where they could convey a clear musical expression of Ireland at a time when the country was more and more torn internally. The Germans especially loved them. In one interview Luke said: 'They know the songs better than we do, the history and the context. For them it's very much an expression of Irish history. They see it as a very valid expression of what the Irish are.' Life was in some ways less complicated on tour, and The Dubliners were good ambassadors for Ireland in places starved of a genuine folk tradition.

This in itself made it difficult to break out in new directions, because the audiences begged for the old reliables, which meant that Luke was pressed to deliver 'The Wild Rover' or 'Whiskey in the Jar' for the thousandth time with the same unbridled gusto as he had the first. The dilemma is no doubt familiar to all successful musical groups. In one interview on RTE Luke, in a forthright mood about his own restlessness, said: 'It looks as if we could go on as long as we want to stay together. It's like a family. And the relationships vary from day to day. They're constantly shifting. Sometimes somebody's your favourite today; tomorrow he's your greatest enemy. So it trips around. When we're not working we very seldom see each other. We don't socialise together. It's not deliberate, not policy; it's just the way it is. We all live in different parts of the city, and we have different hobbies. For instance, Ronnie's keen on horses, Barney's mad on boats, and I play a bit of golf. John is more of a homebody, very domesticated.

'One of the things that has happened with the group is that we ceased to explore musically quite a long time ago. That I would like to see change. But I think you'd have to have a personnel change for that to happen because we're too set in our ways. The formula that we've worked out seems to have worked, and so we're reluctant to change. '

There is no doubt that he felt constrained. In other circumstances he might have made a more determined effort to return to professional acting or branch out more on his own musically. His interest in exploring popular music was well known. For a short time he was involved in an embryonic pop group called 'The Hoop Throwers' with Bill Whelan, drummer Des Reynolds and John Curran, the flautist and saxophonist. He also made one single of a Kinks' song, 'Thank You For the Days'. His friends and his fellow Dubliners joked that he was equally a frustrated soccer player, since he followed the game avidly to the end of his days, and also a frustrated academic – Jim McCann has described him as 'the precursor to the Open University', because his respect for learning and hunger for knowledge was a driving force that never abated. His book-reading habit expanded into collecting, and he loved to get first editions of old books, especially on political philosophy. He was greatly grieved when a fire on the top floor of his house later detroyed much of his cherished collection.

But the years of constant travel and hard living were beginning to take their toll. In April of 1974 the group suffered their first severe blow when Ciarán Bourke was suddenly taken ill during a show in Eastbourne and rushed to St George's Hospital, where a brain aneurism was diagnosed. His life hung in the balance for several days, and an operation left him partially paralysed. Jim McCann stepped into the breach to take Ciarán's place; but Ronnie Drew, who had always loathed the heavy travel schedule and was deeply affected by what had happened to Ciarán, decided that the time had come for his resignation.

Phil Coulter recognised early signs of deterioration in Luke's health, after the years of late nights, regular drinking, too much smoking and straining on the vocal chords. After Luke suffered a brief bout of illness, Phil invited him to Bundoran, where he had arranged a holiday for his family in late July and early August. He didn't expect Luke to take up the offer, but to his astonishment he turned up with his friend, Tommy Weddick. It was during this period, Phil said, that he got most insight into the real Luke. He found him, as I did and I think many others, the most outgoing and gregarious of men and yet an intensely private person who didn't open up to many people. He admired not only his integrity but also his lack of pretentiousness or piety about what he did. Luke stayed in digs in Bundoran with a Mrs O'Neill who looked after him very well and he spent his time swimming, playing football with the kids, dining with friends and, as always, absorbing every bit of printed matter he could get his hands on.

Alcohol seemed to be the most obvious difficulty. In retrospect, John Sheahan said some of the problems Luke began to exhibit – loss of memory, tardiness, which the rest of the group had put down to drink – may well have been due to the incipient tumour. And indeed in 1980, after his first operation, Luke said much the same himself in one interview: 'I should have known two years ago that something was wrong. I was getting these terrible headaches which I thought was migraine – or a hangover from the night before. They came a couple of times each day and I'd go through hell. I was attending a doctor who knew I had a drink problem at the time and who sent me into hospital to "dry out". As a result of everything I never really went in to have a thorough check-up.'

He did 'dry out', though. In one of two radio interviews he did with Micheál Ó Caoimh in Kilkenny, Luke was asked about the 'drinking image' The Dubliners had attached to them from the start. He answered that it was absolutely true – 'in those days'. Did he resent it? 'Not at all, you couldn't resent it. You couldn't deny it! But everything is exaggerated; we didn't tank up just to go on stage to give that impression, there was nothing like that. But there was a lot of drinking. We spent our time in pubs; we were in the environment, the ambiance of drink all the time. So of course it stuck. But here am I off the drink a year and a half...'

The doctor had frightened him off drink, he admitted cheerfully and added with even more cheerful frankness that while it hadn't been as difficult as he'd expected and he could still go to pubs and parties: 'I don't get much enjoyment out of them any more, because eveybody else is at that lovely level where every joke is hilarious, every song is beautiful. But you're sober and it doesn't sound all that great any more...'

Madeleine Seiler, who lived with Luke in the last years of his life, said that he was frustrated with what he was doing at that time, and would have liked to find a new direction. He valued his privacy increasingly and enjoyed staying at home and, as always, reading. He still loved the theatre, and they went at least once a week to some production; she said the last performance Luke saw before he died was Anne Bushnell's interpretation of Edith Piaf, the great singer from the Parisian slums whom Luke greatly admired. Yet when on tour with The Dubliners in Germany, Madeleine said, Luke liked nothing more than visiting the ordinary bars where he could hold conversations with the locals, with her acting as interpreter. He still had a penchant for an argument, though she found him a thoughtful listener, who could consider points and return to say, 'You're right'. He also acknowledged that much of what he deeply believed in wasn't working in eastern Europe, but in her view he never surrendered his humanistic vision of liberation.

Perhaps more than anybody, Madeleine understood Luke's sense of frustration in those latter years of his life: his unfulfilled ambitions and also his need to achieve an inner peace. She provided an important stability and a calming influence during a period when Luke was experiencing enormous pressure and uncertainty. Madeleine has since become a musical promoter who encourages young artists to find their own individual expression and commercial outlets.

In those Ó Caoimh interviews, which were extremely open and honest, I found Luke much less inclined to parry a question with a joke than he had been in earlier times and much more detached and reflective about his work; in a frame of mind to assess where he had come from, how the music had developed, and perhaps wondering what his own next move should be. He talked of the need to adapt to the huge open-air gigs which were just becoming fashionable, how most of his own favourite songs – the slow, tender airs – were absolutely unsuitable. 'It's impossible to even think about doing "Scorn Not His Simplicity". First of all the song is wrong for that, the audience wouldn't have listened. They would have shown an interest, but being so quiet, so undemonstrative, if you like, they would have lost interest. That kind of song in that situation is probably the wrong thing because the song is devalued…'

But he also pointed out the advantages of different venues for performers. 'You can be spoiled by having everything absolutely quiet, the cathedral hush and all that stuff. In fact, you have to be careful in those situations, because people can hear the bum things that you do. In a way the two run into each other – because if you do a lot of your singing in pubs, you might tend to force the voice, so that when you do get silence you hear the roughness in your voice. You can't get away with as many little tricks as you can in the pub,' he added, laughing. But given a choice, he said, he would always choose the concert hall. 'In the concert hall you learn how good you are. Or how inadequate you might be.'

His enthusiasm for the way music was blossoming in Ireland was a constant theme. The Dubliners were no longer the kings of the airwaves as they once had been, which Luke felt was only right. 'There is a new audience. We've been on the go twenty years now. Even a twenty-year-old today to him or her we would seem like old men.The new groups have taken over....you take Planxty, Dé Danann...they've replaced us in the popular mind, the younger mind. They do get more time but they deserve it...' In a characteristic way, he went on to say: 'And these other groups are doing it so well. I'm envious in a way of the standard and the skill of these groups – I'm glad that we were there in the beginning...the ones who set the standard. But these new groups – what am I saying "new", that sounds very condescending!'

He found more variety, more experimentation in modern performances and was especially interested in the resurgence of songwriting, pointing out that the folk revival of the 1960s had had its influence in an unexpected way, by inspiring creativity of a high standard: 'There's more writing going on, in the traditional mode, if that's not a contradiction in terms.' But there was also much more competition.'I was lucky because I was close to MacColl, so it was almost first preference. But there's so many people singing now, so many good singers. When anyone comes along with a song – Pete St John, say – he has myself, for instance, Jim McCann, Christy Moore, Planxty, Liam Clancy. So you don't get first preference anymore. '

Talking about the past, there is almost a puzzlement in his voice. The Dubliners were unique in their day, he said, and never thought of themselves as being good in the sense of setting themselves against a standard, because there was no other group similar enough to compare themselves with. 'We never thought of it in that sense. We did know we had a unique talent in Ronnie Drew's voice; we did know we had a unique talent in Barney's banjo-playing, because Barney's maybe the best banjo player in the world. But he was the best banjo player before we knew him.'

130

Asked whether he had a song he'd want to be remembered by, Luke replied by telling a story that vividly illustrates those early days, of one of the tours when they landed in Enniscorthy. 'In the afternoon with nothing to do but wait around for the show to start, we were in this boozer on the bridge, playing for our own enjoyment. There was only one other customer, a very nicely dressed gentleman, and he stood there listening to us, and said: 'Very nice, gentlemen, do you mind if I sing a song myself? We said not at all, fire away, expecting it to be, you know, something à la John McCormack, a tenor's song. And he had a beautiful, light tenor voice, of course; and he sang a song none of us had ever heard before, a beautiful song. We were mesmerised by that. This was a real example of collecting without expecting to collect.' Afterward 'Bunclody' became one of Luke's songs; when he sang it in Bunclody he dedicated it to the singer in the boozer on the bridge, a local schoolmaster named Michael J Flannery who'd been visiting Enniscorthy. Luke's 'Bunclody' has always been one of my favourites, because it allows him the scope for expression and style in the ballad idiom.

'The excitability of it all in those days was simply the idea of getting up and playing a guitar and singing your head off and people listening to you. Suddenly you were able to sit around in a quiet little pub and swap songs…and you became aware of the richness of the tradition. Rather than waiting for songs to be written for you, or listening to pop songs on radio, you were actually delving, digging back…it was rich. It was never-ending, really…it was so all so new; it really was exciting.'

Luke had moved on. He was growing in his appreciation of the Irish tradition. Now and again, he said, he still called into O'Donoghue's. 'But it's too crowded now. When you get in you can't get out.' He had found other venues, other places for 'telling jokes and news and singing songs to while the time away…'

'There I was then, in front of 2,000 people in the middle of 'The Town I Loved So Well' when it started. I felt the warning sings...I had this terrible spasm of pain down my left side. I was having difficulty holding the instrument and my speech was going. The words I was singing were coming out in a babble. I was taken off and later went on again to finish the show. I knew it was time to have a really good check up.'

So Luke afterward described the night of 30 June 1980, when the mysterious and painful problems he'd been suffering for a long time, with blackouts and violent headaches, struck him with full force on the stage of the Cork Opera House. The following day his tumour was discovered in Cork Regional Hospital. The hopeful news was that it was on the right side and not the left, in which case an operation might have affected his power of movement and speech. He had a five-hour operation to remove the tumour, which required the replacement of a bone in his temple.

The newspapers reported immediately after the operation that it had been a success; they also reported Noel Pearson as saying it would be a ' considerable time before Mr Kelly would be rejoining the group...it is expected that he will be detained in hospital for some time.' Family, friends and colleagues had been told it took three days for a patient to be lucid after such an operation, but Luke was sufficiently alert after 16 hours to ask the consultant surgeon, Mr Buckley, 'Will I be able to play a bit of oul' golf again?' Two months later he was on stage with the rest of the group in the Olympia theatre, performing an excerpt from *Richard's Cork Leg* at a memorial concert to Alan Simpson, who'd put The Dubliners on stage in the show years earlier.

In the short period Luke was offside, he wasn't forgotten. The Dubliners' followers poured their good wishes on him, from Holland, Germany, Britain; he had hundreds of mass cards from all over Ireland. Journalists kept his name in print by wishing him a speedy recovery; Con Houlihan's review of The Dubliners concert at the Olympia a few days after the operation summed up the warm regard of Kelly fans everywhere: 'Without Luke Kelly they are rather like the Dubs without Brian Mullins or a circus without a strong man...Barney McKenna, brave beyond the call of duty, sings the missing one's songs – and does well, even if it isn't the gospel according to Luke.'

Michael Denieffe's piece in the *Sunday Independent* in September was a welcome back: 'A peal of laughter, laced with the throaty hoarseness that launched countless rollicking singing choruses around the world, rang out across the city bar. Heads turned in smiling recognition of the slight, folksy figure with the craggy face framed by a shock of frizzy curls and a goatee beard. The eyes are as mischievously crinkled as ever and the voice a raucous vocal sawmill. The laugh is infectious, too. In the circumstances, it could even be described as a happy salute to the sheer joy of being alive and well.'

Seeing him then, there seemed no reason not to believe his recovery was complete. He had a scar – twenty-five stitches long – from his right ear to the crown of his head, but the famous hair was growing back to camouflage it. He was himself again, and his voice was, he said happily, 'as if nothing had ever happened.' He gave Mr Buckley and his team credit for saving his life, and, asked whether he had prayed, he answered grinning 'You know, it's a long time since I prayed for anything – and I felt it would be very mean of me to go to Him for help because I was in trouble.'

That autumn Luke was back on tour with The Dubliners, starting with a sell-out concert in Amsterdam before an audience of 3,000; 1,000 had to be turned away. Several months later, back in Dublin at an old stomping ground, Mick McCarthy's Embankment in Tallaght, he was suddenly taken ill again and admitted to the Richmond Hospital. He was discharged within days, but within weeks he became so ill during a tour of

Switzerland that he was sent home and ordered to rest. Paddy Reilly stepped into the breach in the group.

For the most part, Luke was too ill to travel or to socialise as he once had in Dublin's pubs. Friends saw him from time to time in some of the usual haunts – Sheehan's on Chatham Street, or Grogan's, presided over by his great friends, Tommy Smith and the late Paddy O'Brien – and he was polite but more withdrawn, though bent as usual over his pile of newspapers or an open book. Ulick O'Connor wrote that he was reading a biography of Albert Schweitzer, the great missionary and mystic, just before he died, and he also relates an incident very typical of Luke: in those last months, his cheque book was stolen, but Luke refused to go to the police even when it became clear someone was forging his signature. He said that since there were only six cheques left, they might as well be let run out.

In March of 1983 he had his second operation, this time in the Richmond, and though once again his recovery from surgery was swifter than anyone expected, the cumulative toll of pain and suffering was great. A sombre note from the *Sunday Independent* a month later says: ' The legendary Luke Kelly sits in a Dublin city centre pub with a pint of dark Guinness in front of him, uncharacteristically quiet and subdued…he is on sick leave from The Dubliners, with Sean Cannon taking his place for the time being.'

Although he did perform in some concerts with The Dubliners the summer before his death, he spent much more time at home in Ranelagh with his companion Madeleine Seiler. His own local was the Leeson Lounge and some old friends met him there, among them Peggy Jordan, who said they often sat in companionable silence. Luke had been very fond of Peggy's husband, Tom, flying home from New York to visit him when he was dying. 'I remember that once when he asked me how Tom was doing, and whether he was suffering, and I answered, "Ah you know Luke there's suffering that's worse than pain." When Luke was battling with his final illness,' he suddenly said to me one day "Do you remember what you said to me when Tom was dying, that there's suffering that's worse than pain? I know what you mean now".'

Sean Cannon also saw Luke a lot during that summer, visiting quietly in the Leeson. Sean's stories of Luke are reminiscent of Christy Moore's, a record of generosity and encouragement to a singer on the way up. He was once doing a solo gig in a small, out of the way village called Barwell in Leicestershire. 'And as I arrived there a taxi also arrived and out of it stepped Luke. I couldn't believe it. The Dubliners were touring and he had a night off. And he came out to the club and in to give encouragement to myself.' One of the last people to spend time with Luke before his death was the musician and singer, Dara Ó Lochlainn, now sadly also a part of Dublin's past. On the sleeve notes to 'Luke's Legacy', Dara writes: 'At 11 o'clock "of a Tuesday" as they say in Dublin, I found Luke in the Leeson Lounge across from his Dartmouth Square domicile. He was drinking a campari and soda: "whore's drink" was his opinion, leaving the table to return with two pints of Guinness. "That continental gargle is not for me," he said, addressing himself to Arthur G with gusto. It seemed impossible to disassociate the pint from the player. I had called around to offer him a song from my father's collection, "The Thief of the World". We ran through it while he found the chords on the guitar, then he said: 'Ah sure you'd sing it better.' I protested, but he never recorded it. Three weeks later Luke of the Fiery Hair had left us...I remember, as we parted that morning, he roared: "When I go it'll be for a warm shake hands with Auld Nick!" Keep it hot for us, Luke, till I get there.'

Luke was admitted to the Richmond for emergency treatment on Saturday night, 28 January 1984 and died on 30 January shortly after 11 p.m. For days afterward the Dublin papers were full of tributes from musicians, singers, journalists, each with a personal anecdote to tell. John Sheahan organised the music for his funeral, with the assistance of John Curran who wrote a special arrangement for trombones and trumpets of 'The Old Triangle.' The medley included the songs Luke was famous for, and some of his favourites, including a composition of John's called 'The Prodigal Son', which Luke used to introduce on stage, John said, with 'Ladies and Gentleman, Johann Sebastian Sheahan' and a big grin on his face. Barney McKenna and Luke's three brothers carried the coffin covered in wreaths , including a bright red one tied with a green ribbon, with a simple inscription marking a friendship which went back to the days when The Dubliners were on their first tour of Germany. It said: 'From Paul McCartney and Ringo Starr.' The celebrities who crowded into the church in Whitehall for his funeral ranged from political leaders to soccer stars and every area of the performing arts. And though Luke may have felt it would be smallminded to approach God, there were half a dozen clergymen on the altar anxious to intercede on his behalf. I stayed outside the door with some of Luke's old friends, most of whom were never very prominent at the altar rails of any church.

But it was not the number of celebrities or priests that mattered; it was the plain people of Dublin, who considered Luke a personal friend. As Dick Grogan wrote of the removal in *The Irish Times*, 'Luke Kelly's people filled the Church of the Holy Child in Whitehall last night to keep a Dubliner company on the first stage of his final journey: ordinary people, workers, trade unionists, musicians, actors, friends. They thronged the vast, vaulted expanses of one of north Dublin's largest churches and spilled over into the car park outside. Hundreds of cars followed the cortège for the removal of the body from the Richmond Hospital through relentless rain...'

Ronnie Drew noticed a couple of fellows working on

the road outside who came into the church on their tea break to pay their respects and his brother was approached outside the church by a bewildered elderly man who gazed uncomprehendingly at the crowds and asked: 'Excuse me, son, is today a holy day or what?'

According to some, in the last months of his life Luke was most drawn to a song that had been a favourite of his for years, seldom sung but on his compilation album released in 1982. It was called 'The Unquiet Grave':

The wind that blows today, my love,
A few small drops of rain.
I never had but one true love
In cold clay she's lain...

CHAPTER NINE

> The sound of Luke Kelly in full flight was a sound
> not to be missed by anyone with any feeling at all
> for music...he had a quality impossible to define
> and certainly impossible to learn.
>
> Phil Coulter in the *Sunday Folk* tribute on RTE,
> February 1984

The first of Luke's legacies took shape shortly after his death. Over his long weeks in the Richmond Hospital, Luke had characteristically made good friends and taken an interest in the research work being done there, and suggested that The Dubliners might help with fund-raising. He was dead before the idea could be put into action, but The Dubliners got together with Luke's family and senior staff in the Richmond and proposed that a fund in his name should be opened with a launch at the National Concert Hall.

The day before that concert in May 1984, one of Ireland's more acerbic columnists, Kevin Myers, put his tribute into print in *The Irish Times*: 'Now there are in Dublin what are called characters, men who know themselves as characters, who cultivate the style of being characters, and who, when they die, are universally remembered with affection as characters. In life they were in fact bores, loathed by the more perceptive for their presumption that they did not have to buy a round because, why, they were characters and characters are characters whose mere presence is sufficient contribution to the company (which they will not hesitate to abandon the moment a more influential or more prosperous group arrives)...but character is the only word to describe Luke Kelly, in the best and special sense, for he was a greatly loved man. He was a genuine character.'

That genuine character was what gave his voice its power and raw vitality, and the reason Luke had a special significance for so many people. Michael D Higgins, the Labour TD and now Minister for Arts, Culture and the Gaeltacht, described very well the breadth of his vision and interest at the unveiling of the granite memorial on his grave in Glasnevin a year after Luke's death: 'He moved from the world of song and music, through the world of poetry and theatre, to the world of politics in its finest and best sense. He was interested in how one's full talents might be used to express the hurt and the pain of the oppressed and the exploited. To celebrate life without that recognition was a choice he respected. His relationship to folk music and his association with such artists as Ewan MacColl also reflected a commitment that went way beyond singing – a commitment that sought the recovery of history and present experience of those lives at the margin, or below the limits set for them by exploitation and repression.'

Among his fellow artists and musicians, Luke evokes particular memories. Christy Moore said he was drawn into the world of performing ballads by the Clancys, 'and subsequently was drawn in further by the excitement of The Dubliners. I was a fair bit down the road when I became aware of what made Luke special. In 1966 I heard him sing solo in MacColl and Seeger's club in London, which was then regarded as the most influential platform of radical folk songs in Britain. I was amazed by the power and commitment of Luke's performance and of how involved he was emotionally with his material. Like myself, Luke came with a repertoire of songs none of which were self-penned, but in those days this was not deemed to be a failing.

'Circa 1968, Luke befriended me. I was busking a Dubliners' queue outside The Two Brewers pub in Salford where they were shooting a television special. Luke hauled me out of the queue and brought me in. That night he introduced me to anyone around who could further my career, telling them "Listen to this guy – he's good." He showed his generosity to other singers. He was never competitive in the area of songs – always generous – the music was to be shared.

'Later he was to lose some of his edge and I personally believe that the merry-go-round of gigs that The Dubliners embarked upon eroded the sparkle and initiative off them. I know nothing of Luke's politics. I knew him to be a generous man whose good deeds did not need to be announced by PR companies. He was a hero who became a friend and I still mourn him.'

Mary Coughlan, another great singer, put it this way: 'Luke stood out as being passionate in his singing. The Dubliners are thought of as a jolly, good-time band; Luke sang the sadder songs. He put soul into it.'

Frank Harte, assessing Luke's achievement from the ballad and traditional music standpoint, said: 'I'd place Luke on a par with Seosamh Ó hÉanaí or Darach Ó Cathain, or Nioclás Tóibín. He was the eastern element, if you like, of the Irish tradition. That's really where Luke Kelly stands, and he stands head and shoulders above all the others – as Donagh MacDonagh said, we have no allegiance to currach and báinín. Luke gave expression to the social conditions within the city. He gave a voice to the unemployed, he gave a voice to the worker, a voice to the person on the streets of Dublin. That's what Luke did, gave them a strong voice; himself and Brendan Behan. I would put the two of them together.'

His colleagues in The Dubliners have their unique memories of him. For Barney McKenna, 'Luke stood out like a rowan tree. When he sang, he made everybody sit back – or dance.'

John Sheahan said Luke's death 'was like the loss of a brother. We were so long together that we were very close…Luke was a very generous friend. For him, the trappings of success meant very little.' He told me a story to illustrate the point. Visiting Luke in his flat, John was startled to find an elegant inlaid table that matched a set of chairs his wife had bought at an auction. 'Either you take the chairs or I'll have to buy the table,' he said to Luke. 'They belong together.' Almost as soon as he spoke, Luke had the table up and on the roof-rack of John's car, flatly refusing to consider any mention of money.

In all the interviews in the press, and radio and television after Luke's death, The Dubliners paid tribute to their comrade in their very different and inimitable ways, but Ronnie Drew, whose authentic street-singer's voice is still the distinct sound of The Dubliners today, summed it up with that terse line: 'He brooked no falsity.'

Eric Fleming of the Work and Play Band was at one time a waiter in the old Red Bank, the most up-market restaurant in Dublin at a time before we knew the word 'up-market', and served Luke one night at dinner with an august group of promoters. Instead of light banter about the entertainment world, the talk was a heated political debate with Luke more than holding his own, to Eric's great satisfaction. Eric, a fellow trade unionist and brother of Gerry, followed in Luke's footsteps literally, staying in his room in the Mulready home in Birminghan where he too became an adopted son while working in England and serving a musical apprenticeship.

Luke's youngest brother John, an ardent football fan in the family tradition, presents another side of him. Luke was a good player in his own right as well as a lifelong follower of the game. 'He was a good friend of Johnny Giles, who played for Stella Maris when Luke played for Home Farm. When Jack Charleton speaks of the great hooleys after an Irish soccer match, he's referring back to a long-standing tradition which developed from the days when Luke, Paddy Reilly, the Dublin City Ramblers would get together with the team for a celebration, win, lose or draw.'

Con Houlihan has similar memories, and recalled in his memoir his last meeting with Luke at the Leinster

Cup final betwen St Pat's and Drogheda United in Tolka Park about a year before his death. 'That night at Tolka Park we embraced when the final whistle blew – and shed a few tears. Luke is an immortal – the world is better for his presence.'

From the early days when Luke Kelly and The Dubliners led the way, they have been followed by Ireland's singers onto the international stage. Excellent singers – Paul Brady, Christy Moore, Sinead O'Connor, Liam Ó Maonlaí, Bono, Enya, Christy Hennessey, Mary Black, Frances Black, Paddy Reilly, the Fureys, Maura O'Connell, Dolores Keane, Mick Hanly, Chris De Burgh, so many others – all sounding in individual ways a voice for Ireland in the world. Perhaps few of them think of themselves as folk singers, but the influence of a deep Irish tradition is there. Their experience of that tradition has given them an edge in bringing something different to audiences far removed from their backgrounds. What is exciting, and what Luke Kelly would have relished, are the new visions of what Ireland is about – or as Bono put it succinctly in *Bringing It All Back Home*: 'We had this idea of Ireland rammed down our throats. So we threw it up.' In a lot of respects, Ireland's contribution to popular music is comparable to the contibution Irish writers made to the literature in the English language. What we lack in commercial acumen we seem to make up for with the richness in these arts, and they may be of more relevance and durability in the 21st century as society draws back from the mad, mad world of cut-throat competition and its companions, poverty and social exclusion. When people begin to find time for each other again, these values will regain their place in the scale of things.

The coming together of people to make music, sing and dance has always been a powerful catalyst for unity, and also a means of discerning and appreciating what was worth keeping or discarding from the past. Music links people; old labels give way to the common joy of being alive. That great impetus for social change in the '60s had potential that was buried by events but it is still there. Journalist Sean MacConnell, who comes from one of the most musical families in Ireland, gave me a memory of Luke that makes that point: 'The first time I met Luke Kelly was over thirty years ago at an Ulster fleadh cheoil in Cootehill. We MacConnells always travelled in a pack, a real clan, my father Sandy, my mother Mary, Cathal, Micky, my sister Maura and myself.

'Dubliners were an exotic enough species, especially bearded Dubliners in blue denim, at Ulster fleadhs, but Luke soon broke through any reserves that might have existed and in no time at all there was a fine session. Luke had an amazing knowledge of traditional songs, even Ulster ones that we used to hold close to our chests and only let out when under severe pressure. I remember the session very well, because we were joined at one stage by Tommy Makem and his mother, Sara, a fine singer from Lisnaskea, Co Fermanagh; Tommy McDermot and Bean MacEntee, a schoolteacher from Fourmilecross, Monaghan.

'Kelly did a lot that night to rectify the image of Dubliners with the traditional musicians who were still wary over the disruption in Mullingar at the All-Ireland fleadh not long before. Here was a guy who looked as if he could start and finish a riot, yet he spoke our kind of language and loved the music as much as we did.

'Over the years I have seen traditional music unite all classes and breeds, all colours and creeds of people. Ours was a music house going back to the 1950s; that was long before publicans discovered there was money in music. I can go back to a time when traditional music was only appreciated by the poor, who kept it alive. My parents made it a rule that the house was open to anyone of any creed who loved the music and for many years, especially during the troubles in the North, my home provided a safe haven for musicians, especially Belfast musicians who would have found difficulty playing at home. On many occasions I saw Shankill Road men rub shoulders with Falls Road people and the Presbyterians from the glens of Antrim play happily with republicans from Cork or Galway. There was never a hard word, though the subject of politics was avoided like the plague.

'It would be unfair to pick out individual people or to name them, but suffice it to say that when my mother died two years ago, many of those people came to bury her, including one man who confessed to me that but for the memories of those days and the way my parents ran their home, he would never have put his foot inside 'a Popish preaching house.'

In a sense, we are far more able to communicate through plays and poetry, song and music, than to speak to each other clearly and without menace. Our old friend Mick McCarthy of the Embankment – and later, the Lady Gregory – said at Luke's grave: 'No voice and no music more clearly represented the feelings of a generation: feelings of resentment against injustice, of "man's inhumanity to man"…I have no doubt whatsoever that The Dubliners, Ewan MacColl, Peggy Seeger and a few American groups and artistes had an influence not yet fully realised or appreciated in bringing about the vast improvement we see today in the world climate. This in turn will speed the day we all long for: peace and harmony in our own troubled island.'

And in the meantime, there is a bridge in Dublin, a fitting memorial for a man who in his day bridged many a divide. A few months after Luke's death, Tony Gregory, TD and Dublin councillor, proposed that the rejuvenated Ballybough bridge across the Tolka should be named after him. Putting the motion to the council, Tony pointed out that Luke had grown up in the area and never lost touch with its people: 'He epitomised the people of the city.' Support was unanimous across the party lines.

But of course not everyone was pleased, as Luke would have been amused but not surprised to learn. According to a report in *The Irish Times*, there was a number of angry complaints to Dublin Corporation about the decision. 'The main objections appeared to have been that his status as a ballad singer and his liking for the pint of Guinness were not sufficient qualities to warrant a bridge being named after him. The complainants felt it was demeaning the community and not doing an awful lot for the new bridge...' A Corporation spokesman said if they were to go by the 'image', they would have to drop the Brendan Behan fellowship.

On 30 May 1984, the bridge was formally opened by the then Lord Mayor, Mick O'Halloran, with The Dubliners in full play. So Luke became a part of the physical history of Dublin, and in a manner that would suit the boy who liked Irish history at St Laurence O'Toole's in Sheriff Street: a bridge has spanned that particular spot on the Tolka since 1313.

We need more bridges in this society. We Dubliners were lucky to have had Luke Kelly, and to share in the celebration and meaning of his life. He was about what Joe Hill and other great socialists were about, as so often proclaimed in Luke's voice in full flight:

I dreamed I saw Joe Hill last night,
Alive as you and me.
Said I but Joe, you're ten years dead,
I never died, said he; I never died, said he.

An Fear Rua
(Ómós do Luke Kelly)

Declan Collinge

Thar chleatráil an ollstóir
Thar ghiob geab mo pháistí
Réabann do ghuth chugham le fórsa
Is is deachair a chreidiúint
Nach maireann tú.

Blaisim arís seirbhe
Mo chéad phionta
i measc na leaids
Is chím arís thú
Sa spotsholas faoi lán seoil
I measc do bhuíne
Cos ghiortach ort ag preabadh
Le rithim an bhainseó
D'fholt rua casta
is do mheigeall rábach
Ag cur led bhruth.

chanamar and port
An uair sin
Is ligeamar gártha molta,
Sinn mórtasach as ár n-óige
As ár n-urlabhraí
Is as ár gcathair araon.
Ba thusa riamh
Fear na cúise
Fear na haislinge
Fear an cheoil
Rábaire tréithiúil

Na huaire.
Caitear do mhacalla chugam
Thár ghlór an tslua
Thár rírá na scuainí fada
Thár ghlór tomhaiste na ríomhairí
Is má bhrúchtann cnap
Im scornach, a Luke,
Ní tusa amháin a chaoinim
Ach port seinnte ár gcathrach
Is glúin aerach dhócasach.

THE RED-HAIRED MAN
(A tribute to Luke Kelly)

('An Fear Rua' translated from the Irish by the poet)

Over the clatter of the supermarket
Over the prattle of my children
Your voice comes forcefully to me
And it is hard to believe
That you are dead.

Once more I taste the sourness
Of my first pint
Among the lads
And I see you again
In the spotlight in full flight
Among your crew,
Your short leg beating time
To the rhythm of your banjo
Your red curly shock
And your brazen goatee
Enhancing your power.

We sang our songs
That night
And roared our applause
Proud of our youth
Of our spokesman
And of our city alike.

You were ever
A man of causes,
A man of vision,
Of music,
Talented champion
Of the hour.

Your echo comes back to me
Above the din of the crowd
Above the clamour of the queues
Above the measured voice of the registers.
And my throat fills up, Luke,
It is not you alone that I lament
But the lost song of our city
And a reckless generation.

From *Faoi Léigear* (Coiscéim, 1990)

LUKE: A TRIBUTE

A ballad by Micheál Ó Caoimh

The years have passed, the time has flown
Since first I saw you there
With feet apart to the music moved,
Your bright red curling hair
The spotlights shone in colour bright
Reflecting on your face
The music notes soared sweet and clear
In the spirit of your race.

Your songs told tales of peace and joy
Of sorrow and of love
The power and passion of your voice
Soared heavenly above
And from the inner soul and heart
With emotion in each song
You stirred the hearts of many, Luke,
When you sang of right and wrong.

The humour in those laughing eyes
Was shared in full with all
When you chose a song to lift the hearts
That filled the music hall
The ecstasy and joy was felt
In chorus, clap and cheer
When that 'son of Róisín' took the stage
The king of balladeers

I saw you sing a thousand times
Ten thousand songs or more
I still can clearly hear you sing
Though your time with us is o'er
For memories now are all we have
When we think of you today
Your name we'll always honour Luke
We're glad you passed this way.

INDEX

Index of Songs and Albums of Luke Kelly and The Dubliners

Other Albums by Luke Kelly and The Dubliners

The Luke Kelly Album; Scorn Not His Simplicity; Luke's Legacy; The Luke Kelly Collection; Ballads and Booze; Twenty Original Hits Vols 1 and 2; *The Dubliner's Collection; The Dubliners — 15 Years.*